College Football Recruiting Handbook

A Parent and Prep's Guide to Earning a College Football Scholarship

Dr. Joe Hornback

Forward by Jeremy Crabtree, ESPN Senior Writer

ISBN-13: 978-1517146795
ISBN-10: 1517146798

Table of Contents

Forward

You have more college football scholarship offers than anybody else has ever had at your high school. Your mailbox overflows with so much mail from programs from coast-to-coast that your family becomes best friends with the mailman. Everywhere you go in town, you're dogged with constant questions about where you're going to school at. You've got so many direct messages from recruiters – and from fans – begging you to come visit your school, it's impossible to keep up with texts from your friends.

Life should be easy, right? It isn't, thanks to the topsy-turvy world of football recruiting.

But it's not too late to change that.

You rack up better stats than the five-star recruit that gets all the headlines in your league. You went to all the camps and combines and tested off the charts, but you watched as somebody else got ushered over to the golf cart with the head coach. You wait by the phone nightly waiting for somebody, anybody, to call and talk to you about playing football for their school, but the phone never rings.

Life isn't fair, right? It isn't, thanks to the topsy-turvy world of football recruiting.

But it's not too late to change that.

No matter if you're the five-star that has everybody in the country beating down their door or the sleeper recruit that is still searching for their first scholarship offer, the recruiting process can be both exhilarating and exasperating at the same time. The same is true if you're a seasoned veteran of recruiting and have been through the process a 100 times or a single-parent that has more questions than answers.

You need a playbook to win the recruiting process, and there is no better resource than this book.

Joe Hornback takes you through the ins and outs of recruiting like nobody else can, because he's been immersed in the process for more than 20 years as a recruit himself, as a player hosting prospects on official visits, as a successful high school coach that had a number of his players go through the process and most recently as an administrator focused on ensuring recruits were academically ready for the next level. He's also spoken to and counseled thousands of prospects and their families over the past decade, as the keynote speaker at recruiting events all over the country.

His playbook will help you answer so many of recruiting's most difficult issues like what to say to a coach when he tries to pressure you to commit when you're not ready, what you and your family can do to help you get the proper exposure you deserve, or how to understand the new world of cost of attendance. Following his advice can turn the process into a blessing, instead of a burden.

Where you go to college will be the second-biggest decision you make in your life, other than who you marry. As a parent, you owe it to your son to guarantee he is armed with the right information to make an informed decision. As a recruit, you should understand the process is something that will define you for the rest of your life. Covering recruiting for the past 20 years, I have seen too many lives ruined by somebody picking a school because they had the best chicken nuggets or prettiest girls, or they didn't get the attention they deserved, or the buckled under the pressure recruiting creates.

This book can ensure you or your son doesn't fall into the same pitfalls as many that have come before. It can change your life, if you're willing to run the plays.

Jeremy Crabtree
Senior Writer at ESPN

Chapter 1
Introduction

My dad was a bricklayer. My mom was a nurse. I am the fourth of five kids in a typical American working class family. Mom and Dad divorced when I was six years old. Money has been tight in my family for as long as I can remember. Mom insisted on a Catholic education, so any college money I could have had was spent on grade school and high school. I wanted to go to college, I didn't have any money, my family did not have any money, I needed a football scholarship.

I was a good high school football player. Prior to my sophomore year, I was called up to the varsity and started the first couple of games at right tackle. Following the third game of the season my coaches asked me to try playing center. I was a little apprehensive until my o-line coach pulled me aside and said, "Joe, you're 6'2" and you're not tall enough to go to the next level as a tackle. This could be your ticket." I was sold. I would watch college games and see guys like Michigan's 6'6" Jumbo Elliott. On Sundays I would watch NFL games and see huge guys like Anthony Munoz, Tony Boselli, and Orlando Pace. I knew I would never be one of those guys.

In college they say that center is the last stop before the bus stop. That was our joke anyway. We would recruit a guy to play defensive line and if he couldn't make plays they would move him to o-line. Usually they would start him out as a tackle, but if he couldn't master a pass set and kept getting smoked on the edge, they would move him to guard. If he had trouble pulling, they moved him to center. If he couldn't play center, he got a bus ticket. I was a sophomore in high school and I was already playing center.

After my junior football season the recruiting process started for me. I was named second team all-state in Iowa's largest classification and I started to get letters from colleges. With every letter I received I got a little more arrogant. Some guys could handle the attention from colleges and not let it get to their head. I was not one of those guys. I believed every college was going to offer me a scholarship and I could go anywhere in the country. In my mind, every college would be lucky to have me, but only one was going to be lucky enough to get me.

All of that changed one night in December during my senior year. I decided that I would go to the University of Iowa. There was only one problem; they had not offered me a scholarship yet. In my mind, a minor detail that would soon be resolved. I was first team all-state my senior year, I had been named in most magazines as one of the top players in Iowa, I was sure I was going to get an offer from Iowa, and if they were lucky, I would take it. I learned a hard lesson that night. The coach who had been recruiting me called me as I was watching television. I answered the phone and we went through our normal routine that we had covered in so many other conversations. He had called me at least 25 times over the last year. Dave Triplett was his name and I had enjoyed talking to him each time he called. "Trip, are you guys going to offer me a scholarship? When am I going to take my visit?"

"Well Joe, that is what I am calling about. I don't think we are going to able to do anything."

I was shocked. I had started to tell people I was going to go to Iowa. When other coaches would call I had started to have my family members screen my calls. I had visited Iowa State the previous weekend and it did not go well. I did not have a D-I offer yet and I was starting to panic. How could this happen to me? I was sure it was going to work out and I didn't have a back-up plan.

The next day, a coach from the University of Kansas, Tim Phillips, visit me at my high school. My attitude had changed dramatically. I sat down with Coach Phillips and asked him a million questions. What was the team like? Where was the University of Kansas? What would I need to bring? How far away was it? I wanted to know all that I could about my new favorite school. We talked for at least two hours about everything. He told me about the stadium, the academics, the new facilities they were building. He told me about how the equipment managers wash everything each day and how I would not have to do my football laundry anymore. He told me about the coaches, the players, the alumni, the secretaries. He did a great job of selling the program and I was eager to buy.

We set up my visit that day for the second week in January. I started taking all of my calls and I set up another visit for Colorado State for the third weekend in January. With Iowa and Iowa State out of the picture I knew I was going to go out of state and that was a little scary. In the meantime, I was getting bombarded by fans of each local school telling me about how I should go to their school. Hawkeye fans bragged about Hayden Fry and what a great coach he would be to play for. Cyclone fans kept telling me about how they needed me and how I could play sooner if I went there. I didn't have the courage to tell them that neither school wanted me and I was in scramble mode.

Thankfully, I loved the University of Kansas. They flew me from Des Moines to Kansas City and my future position coach, Golden Pat Ruel, picked me up at the airport and drove me to from KCI to Lawrence, Kansas. Looking back now it seems a little silly to fly to Kansas City from Des Moines. The flight was only about 30 minutes and you can drive it in three hours, but that is part of recruiting. I enjoyed Coach Ruel right away and he seemed like a nice man from the start. We talked on the entire 45 minute ride from the airport to campus. When we arrived at the football facility I was paired with a current player to be my host for the weekend. Keith Lonecar was an All-Big 8 offensive tackle and he made me feel comfortable right away. He took me around all weekend and took me to some parties, introduced me to the guys on the team, and made me feel important. I remember feeling special because they had paired me with such a good player. When I had gone to Iowa State a few weeks earlier they had paired me with their punter. We had gone to the same high school so I see why they did it, but it felt a lot better when they put me with one of their star players. On my visit I liked the players, I loved the campus, and when you go to a basketball game in Allen Fieldhouse you can't imagine wanting to go to college anywhere else. I had found a home.

On Sunday of my visit I met with Glen Mason, the head coach. It was at Alvamar Country Club after my dad and I finished eating breakfast. Coach Mason came in and sat at our table and started talking to me and dad about how much they liked me and how he wanted me to consider going to school there. I can still remember like it was yesterday when he said, "We want you to come to Kansas. If you do we will pay for your tuition, room, board, books, fees, everything." I was sold. I didn't have a lot of options at the time and I knew that when I told him I was in, my life would change forever, and it did.

As a college football player, I was very average. I was red-shirted my first year. My second year I played in only one game, versus Ball State, and it was at guard. Later in the season I worked my way up to second team and I started to travel with the team. We were competitive good that year and we won eight games and got to go to Hawaii that year and play in the Aloha Bowl. Christmas in Hawaii is a pretty good deal if you ever get a chance and it is something I will always remember.

The following year I was still a backup going into the first game of the season. We were playing Florida State in the Kick-Off Classic in Giants Stadium in New Jersey against the eventual national champions that year and Heisman Trophy winner Charlie Ward. We were overmatched and the 0-49 score further punctuated that point. About mid-way through the first quarter our starting center came limping out. He had been nursing a bad ankle all week and I was secretly hoping he would tweek it so I could get into the game. I can remember running into the game grinning ear to ear. I was playing on national television versus the eventual national champions, and Keith Jackson was doing the game. He even said, "Joe Hornback is now in the game at center for the Jayhawks." My mom taped it, I still have it.

I played 46 snaps that day. It took 50 to letter at Kansas at the time so I remember thinking, "What if I don't get in again this year." I had only played four snaps the year before and I remember preparing my appeal in case it didn't work out. Over the next three games, I started two of them and played in every game the rest of the year once the starter got back. I was named to the Academic All-Big 8 team after the season and the coaches selected me as the "Rookie of the Year" and gave me a plaque.

The following spring I was the starter. The guy in front of me had graduated and I was set to be the man. However, in spring football that year, I hurt my back one day at practice. It was an outside zone play we had run a million times when all of a sudden I felt a numbness go down both legs, my chest tightened and I couldn't breath. I herniated two disks in my back. I tried all kinds of things to make it better. I did countless injections and therapies before finally have surgery in April of that year. I was never the same player after my injury. Any flexibility and speed I had before was gone. When I tried to come back the following fall I was slow, I played high, and the pain never went away, but that wasn't the worst part. For the first time since I started playing as a 6th grader, I was worried about getting hurt again, and everybody knows that if a guy is worried about getting hurt, he will get hurt. Sure enough, I re-injured it that fall in a blocking drill, the second herniation was worse than the first. I was looking at my second back surgery and I had just turned twenty-one. My career was over.

I was granted a medical release and allowed to keep my scholarship. I remember walking into Coach Mason's office and thanking him for giving me a scholarship and a chance. He told me he knew I wanted to be a coach and offered to let me be a student assistant. I tried that for awhile but it was hard to be around the team and not play.

I graduated the following spring with a Bachelor of Science in Education. I was the first one in my family to finish college. I still had a year of student teaching and classes to go before I would be a certified teacher so I started taking graduate classes at night and during the summer. The following fall I did my student teaching at a middle school near Lawrence. In addition, I got my first experience as a real football coach working with the Eudora Middle School 7th Grade fighting Cardinals. I was not in Giants Stadium anymore. I did two student teaching stints to complete my program, one six week stint in middle school and another fourteen week one in a high school. My football scholarship paid for all of it. I realized this gravy train was not going to last forever so I started taking as many classes as I could. I started my masters' project and did my research while I was doing my high school student teaching. When I finished my fifth year I had a Masters Degree in Education. My advisor told me at the time that he could not remember another student doing what I did. In one football scholarship I now had two degrees, but I was not done yet.

During my fifth year while I was student teaching, our director of football operations called me one day and asked me if I was interested in going to graduate school. He told me that Hitachi offered a fellowship to student-athletes in education to continue their career in education. He helped me apply for it and I was granted a $5000 fellowship that I used to get a second Masters Degree in School Administration. I had three degrees and it did not cost me a dime. My football scholarship changed my life. I know the power it has and the advantage it gives a person wanting to get an education.

My first job was at St. Thomas Aquinas High School as teacher and assistant football coach. At the completion of my first season the head coach resigned. He took a job outside the building with the Archdiocese. He called me into his office after he resigned and asked me to help our senior players at the time get recruited. He figured that since I had just got out of college I would know how it worked. I relied on my experience and did the best I could, but the truth be told I didn't know much about it at all. He gave me a rolodex of business cards and asked me to meet with each player and ask him where he wanted to play and start making calls. So that's what I did. I learned right away that everybody wants to play D-I football. Very few guys dream of playing D-II or D-III if they didn't have an older brother play there, or live in a town of one of those schools. On the other hand, all of them want to play at Michigan, Notre Dame, Nebraska, Miami, etc... I understood that because that was how I was when I was in their place five years earlier. Fortunately, we were able to get all of those guys placed in schools they were happy to go to. We had four guys sign that year, one D-I and three D-II.

We hired a new head coach and I stayed one more year before accepting a new teaching job and head coaching position at Grandview High School in Grandview, Missouri. After four years there, I moved back to my hometown of Des Moines, Iowa to be the head football coach at Roosevelt High School for the next five years. In 2007, I left coaching and moved into school administration at Bonner Springs High School in Bonner Springs, Kansas. In eleven years as a high school football coach I helped 43 kids get football scholarships. In nine years as a principal I've been able to see the recruiting process of many athletes in multiple sports. Over the last twenty years I've seen athletic scholarships change lives. I am passionate about recruiting because I've seen firsthand the power it can have in a young person's life. National signing day has become one of my favorite days of the year because I know how an athletic scholarship will change your life. A football scholarship allows a young man to enter into a new chapter that will include him choosing a career, possibly meeting his future wife, and changing where he will live the rest of his life.

In this book I will take you through the recruiting process and cover every facet of recruiting. I will share with you the NCAA rules, what I have learned along the way as a high school player going through the process, a college player hosting recruits, a high school football coach helping athletes, and a high school principal overseeing the process for all sports. Like most things in life there is a right way and a wrong way to handle it. My goal is to help you understand how this process works and help you create as many opportunities as possible so that next year on national signing day you feel good about your decision.

The first thing that is helpful to understand is what the differences are between the different divisions of the NCAA. In D-I there are 128 schools that can each have a maximum of 85 scholarships, assuming they are not on probation with the NCAA for a rules violations and have all of their scholarships to offer. A D-I school can only offer a full scholarship. It is all or nothing. They don't offer partial deals like books only, or tuition only, it's all or nothing. The schools that are currently classified as D-I are:

ACC

School	Nickname	City	State
Boston College	Eagles	Chestnut Hill	Massachusetts
Clemson	Tigers	Clemson	South Carolina
Duke	Blue Devils	Durham	North Carolina
Florida State	Seminoles	Tallahassee	Florida
Georgia Tech	Yellow Jackets	Atlanta	Georgia
Louisville	Cardinals	Louisville	Kentucky
Miami (FL)	Hurricanes	Coral Gables	Florida
NC State	Wolfpack	Raleigh	North Carolina
North Carolina	Tar Heels	Chapel Hill	North Carolina
Pittsburgh	Panthers	Pittsburgh	Pennsylvania
Syracuse	Orange	Syracuse	New York
Virginia	Cavaliers	Charlottesville	Virginia
Virginia Tech	Hokies	Blacksburg	Virginia
Wake Forest	Demon Deacons	Winston-Salem	North Carolina

American

Cincinnati	Bearcats	Cincinnati	Ohio
Connecticut	Huskies	Storrs	Connecticut
East Carolina	Pirates	Greenville	North Carolina
Houston	Cougars	Houston	Texas
Memphis	Tigers	Memphis	Tennessee
Navy	Midshipmen	Annapolis	Maryland

SMU	Mustangs	University Park	Texas
South Florida	Bulls	Tampa	Florida
Temple	Owls	Philadelphia	Pennsylvania
Tulane	Green Wave	New Orleans	Louisiana
Tulsa	Golden Hurricane	Tulsa	Oklahoma
UCF	Knights	Orlando	Florida

Big 12

Baylor	Bears	Waco	Texas
Iowa State	Cyclones	Ames	Iowa
Kansas	Jayhawks	Lawrence	Kansas
Kansas State	Wildcats	Manhattan	Kansas
Oklahoma	Sooners	Norman	Oklahoma
Oklahoma State	Cowboys	Stillwater	Oklahoma
TCU	Horned Frogs	Fort Worth	Texas
Texas	Longhorns	Austin	Texas
Texas Tech	Red Raiders	Lubbock	Texas
West Virginia	Mountaineers	Morgantown	West Virginia

Big Ten

Illinois	Fighting Illini	Champaign	Illinois
Indiana	Hoosiers	Bloomington	Indiana
Iowa	Hawkeyes	Iowa City	Iowa
Maryland	Terrapins	College Park	Maryland
Michigan	Wolverines	Ann Arbor	Michigan
Michigan State	Spartans	East Lansing	Michigan
Minnesota	Golden Gophers	Minneapolis	Minnesota
Nebraska	Cornhuskers	Lincoln	Nebraska
Northwestern	Wildcats	Evanston	Illinois
Ohio State	Buckeyes	Columbus	Ohio
Penn State	Nittany Lions	State College	Pennsylvania
Purdue	Boilermakers	West Lafayette	Indiana
Rutgers	Scarlet Knights	Piscataway	New Jersey
Wisconsin	Badgers	Madison	Wisconsin

8

C-USA

Charlotte	49ers	Charlotte	North Carolina
FIU	Panthers	Miami	Florida
Florida Atlantic	Owls	Boca Raton	Florida
Louisiana Tech	Bulldogs	Ruston	Louisiana
Marshall	Thundering Herd	Huntington	West Virginia
Middle Tennessee	Blue Raiders	Murfreesboro	Tennessee
North Texas	Mean Green	Denton	Texas
Old Dominion	Monarchs	Norfolk	Virginia
Rice	Owls	Houston	Texas
Southern Miss	Golden Eagles	Hattiesburg	Mississippi
UTEP	Miners	El Paso	Texas
UTSA	Roadrunners	San Antonio	Texas
Western Kentucky	Hilltoppers	Bowling Green	Kentucky

Independent

Army	Black Knights	West Point	New York
BYU	Cougars	Provo	Utah
Notre Dame	Fighting Irish	South Bend	Indiana

MAC

Akron	Zips	Akron	Ohio
Ball State	Cardinals	Muncie	Indiana
Bowling Green	Falcons	Bowling Green	Ohio
Buffalo	Bulls	Buffalo	New York
Central Michigan	Chippewas	Mount Pleasant	Michigan
Eastern Michigan	Eagles	Ypsilanti	Michigan
Kent State	Golden Flashes	Kent	Ohio
Miami (OH)	RedHawks	Oxford	Ohio
NIU	Huskies	DeKalb	Illinois
Ohio	Bobcats	Athens	Ohio
Toledo	Rockets	Toledo	Ohio
Western Michigan	Broncos	Kalamazoo	Michigan
Massachusetts	Minutemen	Amherst	Massachusetts

Mountain West

Air Force	Falcons	Colorado Springs	Colorado
Boise State	Broncos	Boise	Idaho
Colorado State	Rams	Fort Collins	Colorado
Fresno State	Bulldogs	Fresno	California
Hawai'i	Rainbow Warriors	Honolulu	Hawai'i
Nevada	Wolf Pack	Reno	Nevada
New Mexico	Lobos	Albuquerque	New Mexico
San Diego State	Aztecs	San Diego	California
San Jose State	Spartans	San Jose	California
UNLV	Rebels	Las Vegas	Nevada
Utah State	Aggies	Logan	Utah
Wyoming	Cowboys	Laramie	Wyoming

PAC-12

Arizona	Wildcats	Tucson	Arizona
Arizona State	Sun Devils	Tempe	Arizona
California	Golden Bears	Berkeley	California
Colorado	Buffaloes	Boulder	Colorado
Oregon	Ducks	Eugene	Oregon
Oregon State	Beavers	Corvallis	Oregon
Stanford	Cardinal	Stanford	California
UCLA	Bruins	Los Angeles	California
USC	Trojans	Los Angeles	California
Utah	Utes	Salt Lake City	Utah
Washington	Huskies	Seattle	Washington
Washington State	Cougars	Pullman	Washington

SEC

Alabama	Crimson Tide	Tuscaloosa	Alabama
Arkansas	Razorbacks	Fayetteville	Arkansas
Auburn	Tigers	Auburn	Alabama
Florida	Gators	Gainesville	Florida
Georgia	Bulldogs	Athens	Georgia
Kentucky	Wildcats	Lexington	Kentucky
LSU	Tigers	Baton Rouge	Louisiana
Mississippi State	Bulldogs	Starkville	Mississippi
Missouri	Tigers	Columbia	Missouri
Ole Miss	Rebels	Oxford	Mississippi
South Carolina	Gamecocks	Columbia	South Carolina

Tennessee	Volunteers	Knoxville	Tennessee
Texas A&M	Aggies	College Station	Texas
Vanderbilt	Commodores	Nashville	Tennessee

Sun Belt

Appalachian State	Mountaineers	Boone	North Carolina
Arkansas State	Red Wolves	Jonesboro	Arkansas
Georgia Southern	Eagles	Statesboro	Georgia
Georgia State	Panthers	Atlanta	Georgia
Idaho	Vandals	Moscow	Idaho
Louisiana-Lafayette	Ragin' Cajuns	Lafayette	Louisiana
Louisiana-Monroe	Warhawks	Monroe	Louisiana
New Mexico State	Aggies	Las Cruces	New Mexico
South Alabama	Jaguars	Mobile	Alabama
Texas State	Bobcats	San Marcos	Texas
Troy	Trojans	Troy	Alabama

The next division is D-IAA. There are 125 of these schools that can have a maximum of 63 equivalents. Notice I did not use the word scholarships. An equivalent means different things to different schools. Some schools will have 63 in-state equivalents, some schools have 63 out-of-state equivalents. Some schools are not fully funded. These equivalents can be split among players. Some guys will start out with a partial scholarship and get more money each year as he becomes more valuable to the team. A D-IAA team will have the same number of players or more that a D-I team but they have less scholarship money to give out. A question I encourage my players to ask when talking to a D-IAA coach is, "Are you a fully funded out of state equivalent institution?" It makes them sound smart and it also tells them what school has more money to spend. The schools that are classified D-IAA are:

Big Sky

School	Nickname	City	State
California Poly State U.	Mustangs	San Luis Obispo	California
Eastern Washington U.	Eagles	Cheney	Washington
Idaho State University	Bengals	Pocatello	Idaho
University of Montana	Grizzlies	Missoula	Montana
Montana State University	Bobcats	Bozeman	Montana
Northern Arizona U.	Lumberjacks	Flagstaff	Arizona
U. of Northern Colorado	Bears	Greeley	Colorado
Portland State University	Vikings	Portland	Oregon
California State U. Sacramento	Hornets	Sacramento	California
Southern Utah University	Thunderbirds	Cedar City	Utah
U. of California, Davis	Aggies	Davis	California
Weber State University	Wildcats	Ogden	Utah
University of North Dakota	None	Grand Forks	North Dakota

Big South

Charleston Southern U.	Buccaneers	North Charleston	S. Carolina
Coastal Carolina University	Chanticleers	Conway	S. Carolina
Gardner-Webb University	Runnin' Bulldogs	Boiling Springs	N. Carolina
Kennesaw State University	Owls	Kennesaw	Georgia
Liberty University	Flames	Lynchburg	Virginia
Monmouth University	Hawks	W. Long Branch	New Jersey
Presbyterian College	Blue Hose	Clinton	S. Carolina

Independent

East Tennessee State U	Buccaneers	Johnson City	Tennessee

CAA

University at Albany, SUNY	Great Danes	Albany	New York
University of Delaware	Fightin' Blue Hens	Newark	Delaware
Elon University	Phoenix	Elon	N. Carolina
James Madison University	Dukes	Harrisonburg	Virginia
University of Maine	Black Bears	Orono	Maine
U. of New Hampshire	Wildcats	Durham	N. Hampshire
University of Rhode Island	Rams	Kingston	Rhode Island
University of Richmond	Spiders	Richmond	Virginia
Stony Brook University	Seawolves	Stony Brook	New York
Towson University	Tigers	Towson	Maryland
Villanova University	Wildcats	Villanova	Pennsylvania
College of William & Mary	Tribe	Williamsburg	Virginia

IVY League

Brown University	Bears	Providence	Rhode Island
Columbia University	Lions	New York	New York
Cornell University	Big Red	Ithaca	New York
Dartmouth College	Big Green	Hanover	N. Hampshire
Harvard University	Crimson	Cambridge	Massachusetts
University of Pennsylvania	Quakers	Philadelphia	Pennsylvania
Princeton University	Tigers	Princeton	New Jersey
Yale University	Bulldogs	New Haven	Connecticut

MEAC

Bethune-Cookman University	Wildcats	Daytona Beach	Florida
Delaware State University	Hornets	Dover	Delaware
Florida A&M University	Rattlers	Tallahassee	Florida
Hampton University	Pirates	Hampton	Virginia
Howard University	Bison	Washington	D.C.
Morgan State University	Bears	Baltimore	Maryland
Norfolk State University	Spartans	Norfolk	Virginia
North Carolina A&T	Aggies	Greensboro	N. Carolina
North Carolina Central U.	Eagles	Durham	N. Carolina
Savannah State University	Tigers	Savannah	Georgia
South Carolina State University	Bulldogs	Orangeburg	S.Carolina

Missouri Valley

Illinois State University	Redbirds	Normal	Illinois
Indiana State University	Sycamores	Terre Haute	Indiana
Missouri State University	Bears	Springfield	Missouri
North Dakota State U.	Bison	Fargo	N. Dakota
U. of Northern Iowa	Panthers	Cedar Falls	Iowa
U. of South Dakota	Coyotes	Vermillion	S. Dakota
South Dakota State	Jackrabbits	Brookings	S. Dakota
Southern Illinois	Salukis	Carbondale	Illinois
Western Illinois	Leathernecks	Macomb	Illinois
Youngstown State	Penguins	Youngstown	Ohio

Northeast

Bryant University	Bulldogs	Smithfield	Rhode Island
Central Connecticut State	Blue Devils	New Britain	Connecticut
Duquesne University	Dukes	Pittsburgh	Pennsylvania
Robert Morris University	Colonials	Moon Township	Pennsylvania
Sacred Heart University	Pioneers	Fairfield	Connecticut
Saint Francis University	Red Flash	Loretto	Pennsylvania
Wagner College	Seahawks	Staten Island	New York

Ohio Valley

Austin Peay State	Governors	Clarksville	Tennessee
Eastern Illinois	Panthers	Charleston	Illinois
Eastern Kentucky	Colonels	Richmond	Kentucky
Jacksonville State	Gamecocks	Jacksonville	Alabama
Murray State	Racers	Murray	Kentucky
Southeast Missouri State	Redhawks	Cape Girardeau	Missouri
Tennessee State	Tigers	Nashville	Tennessee
Tennessee Tech	Golden Eagles	Cookeville	Tennessee
U. of Tennessee Martin	Skyhawks	Martin	Tennessee

Patriot League

Bucknell University	Bison	Lewisburg	Pennsylvania
Colgate University	Raiders	Hamilton	New York
Fordham University	Rams	New York	New York
Georgetown University	Hoyas	Washington	D.C.
College of the Holy Cross	Crusaders	Worcester	Massachusetts
Lafayette College	Leopards	Easton	Pennsylvania
Lehigh University	Mountain Hawks	Bethlehem	Pennsylvania

Pioneer

Butler University	Bulldogs	Indianapolis	Indiana
Campbell University	Fighting Camels	Buies Creek	N. Carolina
Davidson College	Wildcats	Davidson	N. Carolina
University of Dayton	Flyers	Dayton	Ohio
Drake University	Bulldogs	Des Moines	Iowa
Jacksonville University	Dolphins	Jacksonville	Florida
Marist College	Red Foxes	Poughkeepsie	New York
Morehead State University	Eagles	Morehead	Kentucky
University of San Diego	Toreros	San Diego	California
Stetson University	Hatters	DeLand	Florida
Valparaiso University	Crusaders	Valparaiso	Indiana

Southern

Tennessee Chattanooga	Mocs	Chattanooga	Tennessee
Furman	Paladins	Greenville	S. Carolina
Mercer	Bears	Macon	Georgia
Samford	Bulldogs	Birmingham	Alabama
The Citadel	Bulldogs	Charleston	S. Carolina
Virginia Military Institute	Keydets	Lexington	Virginia
Western Carolina	Catamounts	Cullowhee	N. Carolina
Wofford College	Terriers	Spartanburg	S. Carolina

Southland

Abilene Christian	Wildcats	Abilene	Texas
Central Arkansas	Bears	Conway	Arkansas
Houston Baptist University	Huskies	Houston	Texas
U. of the Incarnate Word	Cardinals	San Antonio	Texas
Lamar University	Cardinals	Beaumont	Texas
McNeese State	Cowboys	Lake Charles	Louisiana
Nicholls State	Colonels	Thibodaux	Louisiana
Northwestern State	Demons	Natchitoches	Louisiana
Sam Houston State	Bearkats	Huntsville	Texas
Southeastern Louisiana	Lions	Hammond	Louisiana
Stephen F. Austin	Lumberjacks	Nacogdoches	Texas

SWAC

Alabama A & M	Bulldogs	Normal	Alabama
Alabama State	Hornets	Montgomery	Alabama
Alcorn State	Braves	Lorman	Mississippi
Arkansas Pine Bluff	Golden Lions	Pine Bluff	Arkansas
Grambling State	Tigers	Grambling	Louisiana
Jackson State University	Tigers	Jackson	Mississippi
Mississippi Valley State	Delta Devils	Itta Bena	Mississippi
Prairie View A&M	Panthers	Prairie View	Texas
Southern	Jaguars	Baton Rouge	Louisiana
Texas Southern	Tigers	Houston	Texas

The next division is D-II. There are 170 of these schools that can have a maximum of 36 equivalents. The same applies in D-II as it does in D-IAA, the equivalents can be split among players and with only 36 scholarships you don't see very many guys on full football scholarships. Funding is also another good question to ask D-II coaches. They run into the same thing as D-IAA in that not all schools are funded at the rate of an out of state equivalent. Usually what D-IAA and D-II school will do is have a recruit complete a financial aid application and see if the student-athlete qualifies for any type of grant money and put that with their football scholarship offer to create as completive of a package as possible. In addition, some schools are able to offer in-state tuition right away to their athletes as another way of helping to pay for the cost of college. I have had players go to D-II schools for free when they put their federal grant money with football scholarship money. The way I look at it is as long as they don't have to pay it back you can call it whatever you want. The schools that are classified D-II are:

CIAA

School	Nickname	City	State
Bowie State	Bulldogs	Bowie	Maryland
Chowan	Hawks	Murfreesboro	North Carolina
Elizabeth City State	Vikings	Elizabeth City	North Carolina
Fayetteville State	Broncos	Fayetteville	North Carolina
Johnson C. Smith	Golden Bulls	Charlotte	North Carolina
Lincoln University (PA)	Lions	Lower Oxford	Pennsylvania
Livingstone College	Blue Bears	Salisbury	North Carolina
Saint Augustine's	Falcons	Raleigh	North Carolina
Shaw University	Bears	Raleigh	North Carolina
Virginia State	Trojans	Ettrick	Virginia
Virginia Union	Panthers	Richmond	Virginia
Winston–Salem State	Rams	Winston–Salem	North Carolina

GAC

Arkansas Tech	Wonder Boys	Russellville	Arkansas
East Central	Tigers	Ada	Oklahoma
Harding	Bisons	Searcy	Arkansas
Henderson State	Reddies	Arkadelphia	Arkansas
Northwestern Oklahoma	Rangers	Alva	Oklahoma

Ouachita Baptist	Tigers	Arkadelphia	Arkansas
Southeastern Oklahoma	Savage Storm	Durant	Oklahoma
Southern Arkansas	Muleriders	Magnolia	Arkansas
Southern Nazarene	Crimson Storm	Bethany	Oklahoma
Southwestern Oklahoma	Bulldogs	Weatherford	Oklahoma
Arkansas Monticello	Boll Weevils	Monticello	Arkansas

GLIAC

Ashland	Eagles	Ashland	Ohio
Ferris State	Bulldogs	Big Rapids	Michigan
Grand Valley State	Lakers	Allendale	Michigan
Hillsdale College	Chargers	Hillsdale	Michigan
Lake Erie College	Storm	Painesville	Ohio
Malone University	Pioneers	Canton	Ohio
Michigan Tech	Huskies	Houghton	Michigan
Northern Michigan	Wildcats	Marquette	Michigan
Northwood University	Timberwolves	Midland	Michigan
Ohio Dominican	Panthers	Columbus	Ohio
Saginaw Valley State	Cardinals	University Center	Michigan
Tiffin University	Dragons	Tiffin	Ohio
University of Findlay	Oilers	Findlay	Ohio
Walsh University	Cavaliers	Canton	Ohio
Wayne State University	Warriors	Detroit	Michigan

GLVC

Lincoln University (MO)	Blue Tigers	Jefferson City	Missouri
McKendree University	Bearcats	Lebanon	Illinois
Missouri S&T	Miners	Rolla	Missouri
Quincy University	Hawks	Quincy	Illinois
Saint Joseph's College	Pumas	Rensselaer	Indiana
Southwest Baptist	Bearcats	Bolivar	Missouri
Truman State	Bulldogs	Kirksville	Missouri
U. of Indianapolis	Greyhounds	Indianapolis	Indiana
William Jewell College	Cardinals	Liberty	Missouri

GNAC

Azusa Pacific	Cougars	Azusa	California
Central Washington	Wildcats	Ellensburg	Washington
Dixie State	Red Storm	St. George	Utah
Humboldt State	Lumberjacks	Arcata	California
Simon Fraser	Clan	Burnaby	BC
S. Dakota School of Mines	Hardrockers	Rapid City	South Dakota
Western Oregon	Wolves	Monmouth	Oregon

Gulf South

Delta State University	Statesmen	Cleveland	Mississippi
Florida Institute of Tech	Panthers	Melbourne	Florida
Mississippi College	Choctaws	Clinton	Mississippi
Shorter University	Hawks	Rome	Georgia
North Alabama	Lions	Florence	Alabama
West Alabama	Tigers	Livingston	Alabama
West Georgia	Wolves	Carrollton	Georgia
Valdosta State	Blazers	Valdosta	Georgia

Independent

Alderson Broaddus	Battlers	Philippi	West Virginia
Kentucky Wesleyan	Panthers	Owensboro	Kentucky
Limestone College	Saints	Gaffney	South Carolina
North Greenville	Crusaders	Tigerville	South Carolina
Ok Panhandle State	Aggies	Goodwell	Oklahoma
UNC Pembroke	Braves	Pembroke	North Carolina

LSC

Angelo State University	Rams	San Angelo	Texas
Eastern New Mexico	Greyhounds	Portales	New Mexico
Midwestern State	Mustangs	Wichita Falls	Texas
Tarleton State	Texans	Stephenville	Texas
Texas A&M Commerce	Lions	Commerce	Texas
Texas A&M Kingsville	Javelinas	Kingsville	Texas
West Texas A&M	Buffaloes	Canyon	Texas

MEC

Concord	Mountain Lions	Athens	West Virginia
Fairmont State	Falcons	Fairmont	West Virginia
Glenville State	Pioneers	Glenville	West Virginia
Notre Dame College	Falcons	South Euclid	Ohio
Shepherd	Rams	Shepherdstown	West Virginia
University of Charleston	Golden Eagles	Charleston	West Virginia
Virginia's College at Wise	Highland Cavaliers	Wise	Virginia
Urbana University	Blue Knights	Urbana	Ohio
West Liberty University	Hilltoppers	West Liberty	West Virginia
W. Virginia State	Yellow Jackets	Institute	West Virginia
W. Virginia Wesleyan	Bobcats	Buckhannon	West Virginia

MIAA

Emporia State	Hornets	Emporia	Kansas
Fort Hays State	Tigers	Hays	Kansas
Lindenwood	Lions	St. Charles	Missouri
Missouri Southern	Lions	Joplin	Missouri
Missouri Western	Griffons	St. Joseph	Missouri
Northeastern	RiverHawks	Tahlequah	Oklahoma
Northwest Missouri State	Bearcats	Maryville	Missouri
Pittsburg State	Gorillas	Pittsburg	Kansas
U. of Central Missouri	Mules	Warrensburg	Missouri
U. of Central Oklahoma	Bronchos	Edmond	Oklahoma
U. of Nebraska at Kearney	Lopers	Kearney	Nebraska
Washburn	Ichabods	Topeka	Kansas

NE-10

American International	Yellow Jackets	Springfield	Massachusetts
Assumption College	Greyhounds	Worcester	Massachusetts
Bentley	Falcons	Waltham	Massachusetts
Long Island University	Pioneers	Brookville	New York
Merrimack College	Warriors	North Andover	Massachusetts
Pace University	Setters	Pleasantville	New York
Saint Anselm College	Hawks	Goffstown	New Hampshire
Southern Connecticut	Fighting Owls	New Haven	Connecticut
Stonehill College	Skyhawks	Easton	Massachusetts

| University of New Haven | Chargers | West Haven | Connecticut |

NSIC

Augustana College	Vikings	Sioux Falls	South Dakota
Bemidji State	Beavers	Bemidji	Minnesota
Concordia St. Paul	Golden Bears	St. Paul	Minnesota
Min. State Moorhead	Dragons	Moorhead	Minnesota
Minnesota State Mankato	Mavericks	Mankato	Minnesota
Minot State	Beavers	Minot	North Dakota
Northern State	Wolves	Aberdeen	South Dakota
SW Minnesota State	Mustangs	Marshall	Minnesota
St. Cloud State University	Huskies	St. Cloud	Minnesota
University of Mary	Marauders	Bismarck	North Dakota
U. of Min. Crookston	Eagles	Crookston	Minnesota
U. of Minnesota Duluth	Bulldogs	Duluth	Minnesota
U. of Sioux Falls	Cougars	Sioux Falls	South Dakota
Upper Iowa	Peacocks	Fayette	Iowa
Wayne State College	Wildcats	Wayne	Nebraska
Winona State	Warriors	Winona	Minnesota

PSAC

Bloomsburg U. of Penn.	Huskies	Bloomsburg	Pennsylvania
Cal.University of Penn.	Vulcans	California	Pennsylvania
Cheyney U. of Penn.	Wolves	Cheyney	Pennsylvania
Clarion U. of Penn.	Golden Eagles	Clarion	Pennsylvania
E. Stroudsburg U. of Penn.	Warriors	East Stroudsburg	Pennsylvania
Edinboro U. of Penn.	Fighting Scots	Edinboro	Pennsylvania
Gannon University	Golden Knights	Erie	Pennsylvania
Indiana U. of Penn.	Crimson Hawks	Indiana	Pennsylvania
Kutztown U. of Penn.	Golden Bears	Kutztown	Pennsylvania
Lock Haven U. of Penn.	Bald Eagles	Lock Haven	Pennsylvania
Mercyhurst University	Lakers	Erie	Pennsylvania
Millersville U. of Penn.	Marauders	Millersville	Pennsylvania
Seton Hill University	Griffins	Greensburg	Pennsylvania
Shippensburg U. of Penn.	Red Raiders	Shippensburg	Pennsylvania
Slippery Rock U.of Penn.	Slippery Rock	Slippery Rock	Pennsylvania

| West Chester U. of Penn. | Golden Rams | West Chester | Pennsylvania |

RMAC

Adams State	Grizzlies	Alamosa	Colorado
Black Hills State	Yellow Jackets	Spearfish	South Dakota
Chadron State College	Eagles	Chadron	Nebraska
Colorado Mesa University	Mavericks	Grand Junction	Colorado
Colorado School of Mines	Orediggers	Golden	Colorado
Colorado State Pueblo	ThunderWolves	Pueblo	Colorado
Fort Lewis College	Skyhawks	Durango	Colorado
New Mexico Highlands	Cowboys	Las Vegas	New Mexico
Western New Mexico	Mustangs	Silver City	New Mexico
Western State Colorado	Mountaineers	Gunnison	Colorado

SAC

Brevard College	Tornados	Brevard	North Carolina
Carson–Newman	Eagles	Jefferson City	Tennessee
Catawba College	Indians	Salisbury	North Carolina
Lenoir–Rhyne	Bears	Hickory	North Carolina
Mars Hill	Lions	Mars Hill	North Carolina
Newberry College	Wolves	Newberry	South Carolina
Tusculum College	Pioneers	Tusculum	Tennessee
Wingate University	Bulldogs	Wingate	North Carolina

SIAC

Albany State	Golden Rams	Albany	Georgia
Benedict College	Tigers	Columbia	South Carolina
Central State	Marauders	Wilberforce	Ohio
Clark Atlanta	Panthers	Atlanta	Georgia
Fort Valley State	Wildcats	Fort Valley	Georgia
Kentucky State	Thorobreds	Frankfort	Kentucky
Lane College	Dragons	Jackson	Tennessee
Miles College	Golden Bears	Fairfield	Alabama
Morehouse College	Maroon Tigers	Atlanta	Georgia
Paine College	Lions	Augusta	Georgia
Stillman College	Tigers	Tuscaloosa	Alabama
Tuskegee University	Golden Tigers	Tuskegee	Alabama

The final NCAA division is D-III. These schools do not offer athletic scholarships. Any scholarship offer is need based or on academics. The guys that play at this level truly do it for the love of the game. These schools still recruit just like the D-I, D-IAA, and D-II, but they do not give athletic scholarships for playing football. I have guys that have gone on to play at these schools and had great experiences, loved their college experience and loved playing football for their school.

ASC

School	Nickname	City	State
East Texas Baptist	Tigers	Marshall	Texas
Hardin-Simmons	Cowboys	Abilene	Texas
Howard Payne	Yellow Jackets	Brownwood	Texas
Louisiana College	Wildcats	Pineville	Louisiana
Mary Hardin-Baylor	Crusaders	Belton	Texas
Sul Ross State	Lobos	Alpine	Texas

CCIW

Augustana (IL)	Vikings	Rock Island	Illinois
Carthage	Red Men	Kenosha	Wisconsin
Elmhurst	Bluejays	Elmhurst	Illinois
Illinois Wesleyan	Titans	Bloomington	Illinois
Millikin	Big Blue	Decatur	Illinois
North Central	Cardinals	Naperville	Illinois
North Park	Vikings	Chicago	Illinois
Wheaton (IL)	Thunder	Wheaton	Illinois

Centennial

Dickinson	Red Devils	Carlisle	Pennsylvania
Franklin & Marshall	Diplomats	Lancaster	Pennsylvania
Gettysburg	Bullets	Gettysburg	Pennsylvania
Johns Hopkins	Blue Jays	Baltimore	Maryland
Juniata	Eagles	Huntingdon	Pennsylvania
McDaniel	Green Terror	Westminster	Maryland
Moravian	Greyhounds	Bethlehem	Pennsylvania
Muhlenberg	Mules	Allentown	Pennsylvania
Susquehanna	Crusaders	Selinsgrove	Pennsylvania
Ursinus	Bears	Collegeville	Pennsylvania

ECFC

Anna Maria	AMCATS	Paxton	Massachusetts
Becker	Hawks	Leicester	Massachusetts
Castleton State	Spartans	Castleton	Vermont
Gallaudet	Bison	Washington	DC
Husson	Eagles	Bangor	Maine
Mount Ida	Mustangs	Newton	Massachusetts
Norwich	Cadets	Northfield	Vermont
SUNY-Maritime	Privateers	Bronx	New York

Empire 8

Alfred	Saxons	Alfred	New York
Brockport	Golden Eagles	Brockport	New York
Buffalo State	Bengals	Buffalo	New York
Frostburg State	Bobcats	Frostburg	Maryland
Hartwick	Hawks	Oneonta	New York
Ithaca	Bombers	Ithaca	New York
Salisbury	Seagulls	Salisbury	Maryland
St. John Fisher	Cardinals	Pittsford	New York
Utica	Pioneers	Utica	New York

HCAC

Anderson	Ravens	Anderson	Indiana
Bluffton	Beavers	Bluffton	Ohio
Defiance	YellowJackets	Defiance	Ohio
Earlham	Quakers	Richmond	Indiana
Franklin	Grizzlies	Franklin	Indiana
Hanover	Panthers	Hanover	Indiana
Manchester	Spartans	North Manchester	Indiana
Mount St. Joseph	Lions	Cincinnati	Ohio
Rose–Hulman	Engineers	Terre Haute	Indiana

IIAC

Buena Vista	Beavers	Storm Lake	Iowa
Central (IA)	Dutch	Pella	Iowa
Coe	Kohawks	Cedar Rapids	Iowa
Dubuque	Spartans	Dubuque	Iowa
Loras	Duhawks	Dubuque	Iowa
Luther	Norse	Decorah	Iowa
Simpson	Storm	Indianola	Iowa

Wartburg	Knights	Waverly	Iowa

Independent

Alfred State	Pioneers	Alfred	New York
Chicago	Maroons	Chicago	Illinois
Maranatha Baptist	Sabercats	Watertown	Wisconsin
Washington (MO)	Bears	St. Louis	Missouri
Wesley	Wolverines	Dover	Delaware

Liberty

Hobart	Statesmen	Geneva	New York
Merchant Marine	Mariners	Kings Point	New York
Rochester	Yellowjackets	Rochester	New York
RPI	Engineers	Troy	New York
Springfield	Pride	Springfield	Massachusetts
St. Lawrence	Saints	Canton	New York
Union	Dutchmen	Schenectady	New York
Worcester Poly	Engineers	Worcester	Massachusetts

MAC

Albright	Lions	Reading	Pennsylvania
Delaware Valley	Aggies	Doylestown	Pennsylvania
FDU-Florham	Devils	Madison	New Jersey
King's	Monarchs	Wilkes-Barre	Pennsylvania
Lebanon Valley	Flying Dutchmen	Annville	Pennsylvania
Lycoming	Warriors	Williamsport	Pennsylvania
Misericordia	Cougars	Dallas	Pennsylvania
Stevenson	Mustangs	Owings Mills	Maryland
Widener	Pride	Chester	Pennsylvania
Wilkes	Colonials	Wilkes-Barre	Pennsylvania

MASCAC

Bridgewater State	Bears	Bridgewater	Massachusetts
Fitchburg State	Falcons	Fitchburg	Massachusetts
Framingham State	Rams	Framingham	Massachusetts
Mass. Maritime	Buccaneers	Buzzards Bay	Massachusetts
Plymouth State	Panthers	Plymouth	New Hampshire
UMass Dartmouth	Corsairs	North Dartmouth	Massachusetts
Western Connecticut	Colonials	Danbury	Connecticut
Westfield State	Owls	Westfield	Massachusetts
Worcester State	Lancers	Worcester	Massachusetts

MIAA

Adrian	Bulldogs	Adrian	Michigan
Albion	Britons	Albion	Michigan
Alma	Scots	Alma	Michigan
Hope	Flying Dutchmen	Holland	Michigan
Kalamazoo	Hornets	Kalamazoo	Michigan
Olivet	Comets	Olivet	Michigan
Trine	Thunder	Angola	Indiana

MIAC

Augsburg	Auggies	Minneapolis	Minnesota
Bethel	Royals	Arden Hills	Minnesota
Carleton	Knights	Northfield	Minnesota
Concordia	Cobbers	Moorhead	Minnesota
Gustavus Adolphus	Gusties	St. Peter	Minnesota
Hamline	Pipers	St. Paul	Minnesota
St. John's (MN)	Johnnies	Collegeville	Minnesota
St. Olaf	Oles	Northfield	Minnesota
St. Thomas	Tommies	St. Paul	Minnesota

MWC

Beloit	Buccaneers	Beloit	Wisconsin
Carroll (WI)	Pioneers	Waukesha	Wisconsin
Cornell (IA)	Rams	Mount Vernon	Iowa
Grinnell	Pioneers	Grinnell	Iowa
Illinois College	Blueboys	Jacksonville	Illinois
Knox	Prairie Fire	Galesburg	Illinois
Lake Forest	Foresters	Lake Forest	Illinois
Lawrence	Vikings	Appleton	Wisconsin
Macalester	Scots	St. Paul	Minnesota
Monmouth (IL)	Fighting Scots	Monmouth	Illinois
Ripon	Red Hawks	Ripon	Wisconsin
St. Norbert	Green Knights	De Pere	Wisconsin

NACC

Aurora	Spartans	Aurora	Illinois
Benedictine	Eagles	Lisle	Illinois
Concordia (IL)	Cougars	River Forest	Illinois
Concordia (WI)	Falcons	Mequon	Wisconsin
Lakeland	Muskies	Sheboygan	Wisconsin

| Rockford | Regents | Rockford | Illinois |
| Wisconsin Lutheran | Warriors | Milwaukee | Wisconsin |

NCAC
Allegheny	Gators	Meadville	Pennsylvania
Denison	Big Red	Granville	Ohio
DePauw	Tigers	Greencastle	Indiana
Hiram	Terriers	Hiram	Ohio
Kenyon	Lords	Gambier	Ohio
Oberlin	Yeomen	Oberlin	Ohio
Ohio Wesleyan	Battling Bishops	Delaware	Ohio
Wabash	Little Giants	Crawfordsville	Indiana
Wittenberg	Tigers	Springfield	Ohio
Wooster	Fighting Scots	Wooster	Ohio

NEFC
Coast Guard	Bears	New London	Connecticut
Curry	Colonels	Milton	Massachusetts
Endicott	Gulls	Beverly	Massachusetts
Maine Maritime	Mariners	Castine	Maine
MIT	Engineers	Cambridge	Massachusetts
Nichols	Bison	Dudley	Massachusetts
Salve Regina	Seahawks	Newport	Rhode Island
W. New England	Golden Bears	Springfield	Massachusetts

NESCAC
Amherst	Lord Jeffs	Amherst	Massachusetts
Bates	Bobcats	Lewiston	Maine
Bowdoin	Polar Bears	Brunswick	Maine
Colby	White Mules	Waterville	Maine
Hamilton	Continentals	Clinton	New York
Middlebury	Panthers	Middlebury	Vermont
Trinity (CT)	Bantams	Hartford	Connecticut
Tufts	Jumbos	Medford	Massachusetts
Wesleyan	Cardinals	Middletown	Connecticut
Williams	Ephs	Williamstown	Massachusetts

NJAC
College of N. Jersey	Lions	Ewing	New Jersey
Cortland State	Red Dragons	Cortland	New York
Kean	Cougars	Union Township	New Jersey

Montclair State	Red Hawks	Upper Montclair	New Jersey
Rowan	Profs	Glassboro	New Jersey
Southern Virginia	Knights	Buena Vista	Virginia
SUNY-Morrisville	Mustangs	Morrisville	New York
William Paterson	Pioneers	Wayne	New Jersey

NWC

George Fox	Bruins	Newberg	Oregon
Lewis & Clark	Pioneers	Portland	Oregon
Linfield	Wildcats	McMinnville	Oregon
Pacific (OR)	Boxers	Forest Grove	Oregon
Pacific Lutheran	Lutes	Tacoma	Washington
Puget Sound	Loggers	Tacoma	Washington
Whitworth	Pirates	Spokane	Washington
Willamette	Bearcats	Salem	Oregon

OAC

Baldwin-Wallace	Yellow Jackets	Berea	Ohio
Capital	Crusaders	Columbus	Ohio
Heidelberg	Student Princes	Tiffin	Ohio
John Carroll	Blue Streaks	University Heights	Ohio
Marietta	Pioneers	Marietta	Ohio
Mount Union	Purple Raiders	Alliance	Ohio
Muskingum	Fighting Muskies	New Concord	Ohio
Ohio Northern	Polar Bears	Ada	Ohio
Otterbein	Cardinals	Westerville	Ohio
Wilmington	Quakers	Wilmington	Ohio

ODAC

Bridgewater	Eagles	Bridgewater	Virginia
Catholic	Cardinals	Washington	DC
Emory & Henry	Wasps	Emory	Virginia
Guilford	Quakers	Greensboro	North Carolina
Hampden–Sydney	Tigers	Hampden Sydney	Virginia
Randolph–Macon	Yellow Jackets	Ashland	Virginia
Shenandoah	Hornets	Winchester	Virginia
Washington & Lee	Generals	Lexington	Virginia

PAC

Bethany	Bison	Bethany	West Virginia
Carnegie Mellon	Tartans	Pittsburgh	Pennsylvania
Case Western	Spartans	Cleveland	Ohio
Geneva	Golden Tornadoes	Beaver Falls	Pennsylvania
Grove City	Wolverines	Grove City	Pennsylvania
St. Vincent	Bearcats	Latrobe	Pennsylvania
Thiel	Tomcats	Greenville	Pennsylvania
Thomas More	Saints	Crestview Hills	Kentucky
Washington & Jefferson	Presidents	Washington	Pennsylvania
Waynesburg	Yellow Jackets	Waynesburg	Pennsylvania
Westminster (PA)	Titans	New Wilmington	Pennsylvania

SAA

Berry	Vikings	Mount Berry	Georgia
Birmingham-Southern	Panthers	Birmingham	Alabama
Centre	Colonels	Danville	Kentucky
Hendrix	Warriors	Conway	Arkansas
Millsaps	Majors	Jackson	Mississippi
Rhodes	Lynx	Memphis	Tennessee
Sewanee	Tigers	Sewanee	Tennessee

SCAC

Austin	Kangaroos	Sherman	Texas
Southwestern	Pirates	Georgetown	Texas
Texas Lutheran	Bulldogs	Seguin	Texas
Trinity (TX)	Tigers	San Antonio	Texas

SCIAC

Cal Lutheran	Kingsmen	Thousand Oaks	California
Chapman	Panthers	Orange	California
Claremont-Mudd-Scripps	Stags	Claremont	California
La Verne	Leopards	La Verne	California
Occidental	Tigers	Los Angeles	California
Pomona-Pitzer	Sagehens	Claremont	California
Redlands	Bulldogs	Redlands	California
Whittier	Poets	Whittier	California

UMAC

Crown	Storm	St. Bonifacius	Minnesota
Eureka	Red Devils	Eureka	Illinois
Greenville	Panthers	Greenville	Illinois
Iowa Wesleyan	Tigers	Mt. Pleasant	Iowa
MacMurray	Highlanders	Jacksonville	Illinois
Martin Luther	Knights	New Ulm	Minnesota
Minnesota-Morris	Cougars	Morris	Minnesota
Northwestern (MN)	Eagles	Roseville	Minnesota
St. Scholastica	Saints	Duluth	Minnesota
Westminster (MO)	Blue Jays	Fulton	Missouri

USA South

Averett	Cougars	Danville	Virginia
Christopher Newport	Captains	Newport News	Virginia
Ferrum	Panthers	Ferrum	Virginia
Greensboro	Pride	Greensboro	North Carolina
Huntingdon	Hawks	Montgomery	Alabama
LaGrange	Panthers	LaGrange	Georgia
Maryville	Scots	Maryville	Tennessee
Methodist	Monarchs	Fayetteville	North Carolina
NC Wesleyan	Battling Bishops	Rocky Mount	North Carolina

WIAC

UW–Eau Claire	Blugolds	Eau Claire	Wisconsin
UW–La Crosse	Eagles	La Crosse	Wisconsin
UW–Oshkosh	Titans	Oshkosh	Wisconsin
UW–Platteville	Pioneers	Platteville	Wisconsin
UW–River Falls	Falcons	River Falls	Wisconsin
UW–Stevens Point	Pointers	Stevens Point	Wisconsin
UW–Stout	Blue Devils	Menomonie	Wisconsin
UW–Whitewater	Warhawks	Whitewater	Wisconsin

This covers the NCAA institutions. However, the NCAA is not the only governing body for college athletics, there also the National Association of Intercollegiate Athletics. NAIA schools can offer football scholarships just like the NCAA schools can. The rules according to the NAIA website state:

"Assignment of scholarships, grants-in-aid or student loans shall be controlled by the faculty through the regularly constituted committee on student loans and scholarships.

A member institutions of the NAIA shall award no more institutionally-controlled financial aid to the student-athlete than the actual cost of: 1) tuition; 2) mandatory fees, books and supplies required for course in which the student-athlete only, based on official room and board allowance listed in the institutions catalog. Further financial assistance to a student-athlete, other than listed above, by a member institution shall be prohibited."

In my experience most NAIA schools are funded about at the same level as a D-II NCAA school. They split scholarships and athletes usually get more money they longer they are in the program. The NAIA schools are:

Frontier

Carroll College	Fighting Saints	Helena	Montana
College of Idaho	Coyotes	Caldwell	Idaho
Dickinson State	Blue Hawks	Dickinson	N. Dakota
Eastern Oregon	Mountaineers	La Grande	Oregon
Montana State U. Northern	Lights	Havre	Montana
Montana Tech	Orediggers	Butte	Montana
Rocky Mountain College	Battlin' Bears	Billings	Montana
Southern Oregon	Raiders	Ashland	Oregon
Montana Western	Bulldogs	Dillon	Montana

Great Plains

Briar Cliff	Chargers	Sioux City	Iowa
Concordia	Bulldogs	Seward	Nebraska
Dakota Wesleyan	Tigers	Mitchell	S. Dakota
Doane College	Tigers	Crete	Nebraska
Dordt College	Defenders	Sioux Center	Iowa
Hastings College	Broncos	Hastings	Nebraska
Midland University	Warriors	Fremont	Nebraska
Morningside College	Mustangs	Sioux City	Iowa

| Nebraska Wesleyan | Wolves | Lincoln | Nebraska |
| Northwestern College | Red Raiders | Orange City | Iowa |

Heart of America

Avila University	Eagles	Kansas City	Missouri
Baker University	Wildcats	Baldwin City	Kansas
Benedictine College	Ravens	Atchison	Kansas
Central Methodist	Eagles	Fayette	Missouri
Culver-Stockton College	Wildcats	Canton	Missouri
Evangel University	Crusaders	Springfield	Missouri
Graceland University	Yellowjackets	Lamoni	Iowa
MidAmerica Nazarene	Pioneers	Olathe	Kansas
Missouri Valley College	Vikings	Marshall	Missouri
Peru State College	Bobcats	Peru	Nebraska

Independent

Arizona Christian	Firestorm	Phoenix	Arizona
Haskell Indian Nations	Indians	Lawrence	Kansas
Lindenwood	Lynx	Belleville	Illinois
Menlo College	Oaks	Atherton	California
Missouri Baptist	Spartans	St. Louis	Missouri

KCAC

Bethany College	Swedes	Lindsbord	Kansas
Bethel College	Threshers	Newton	Kansas
Friends University	Falcons	Wichita	Kansas
Kansas Wesleyan	Coyotes	Salina	Kansas
McPherson College	Bulldogs	McPherson	Kansas
Ottawa University	Braves	Ottawa	Kansas
Southwestern College	Moundbuilders	Winfield	Kansas
Sterling College	Warriors	Sterling	Kansas
Tabor College	Bluejays	Hillsboro	Kansas
University of Saint Mary	Spires	Leavenworth	Kansas

Mid-South

Belhaven University	Blazers	Jackson	Mississippi
Bethel University	Wildcats	McKenzie	Tennessee
Bluefield College	Rams	Bluefield	Virginia
Campbellsville	Tigers	Campbellsville	Kentucky
Cumberland	Bulldogs	Lebanon	Tennessee

Faulkner University	Eagles	Montgomery	Alabama
Georgetown College	Tigers	Georgetown	Kentucky
Kentucky Christian	Knights	Grayson	Kentucky
Lindsey Wilson College	Blue Raiders	Columbia	Kentucky
Reinhardt University	Eagles	Waleska	Georgia
Union College	Bulldogs	Barbourville	Kentucky
University of Pikeville	Bears	Pikeville	Kentucky
U. of the Cumberlands	Patriots	Williamsburg	Kentucky

Mid-States

Concordia	Cardinals	Ann Arbor	Michigan
Grand View University	Vikings	Des Moines	Iowa
Marian University	Knights	Indianapolis	Indiana
Olivet Nazarene	Tigers	Bourbonnais	Illinois
Robert Morris	Eagles	Chicago	Illinois
Saint Xavier	Cougars	Chicago	Illinois
Siena Heights	Saints	Adrian	Michigan
St. Ambrose	Fighting Bees	Davenport	Iowa
Taylor University	Trojans	Upland	Indiana
Trinity International	Trojans	Deerfield	Illinois
U. of Saint Francis (IN)	Cougars	Fort Wayne	Indiana
U. of St. Francis (IL)	Saints	Joliet	Illinois
William Penn	Statesmen	Oskaloosa	Iowa

Sun

Ave Maria University	Gyrenes	Naples	Florida
Edward Waters College	Tigers	Jacksonville	Florida
Point University	Skyhawks	East Point	Georgia
Southeastern	Fire	Lakeland	Florida
Warner University	Royals	Lake Wales	Florida
Webber International	Warriors	Babson Park	Florida

Central States

Bacone College	Warriors	Muskogee	Oklahoma
Langston University	Lions	Langston	Oklahoma
Oklahoma Baptist	Bison	Shawnee	Oklahoma
SW Assemblies of God	Lions	Waxahachie	Texas
Texas College	Steers	Tyler	Texas
Wayland Baptist	Pioneers	Plainview	Texas

Chapter 2
Recruiting Mail

The first time you get a letter in the mail from a college, you think you have died and gone to heaven. Not everyone gets them so you know you are special because they took the time to put your name on the envelope and send it. You have arrived.

The NCAA allows colleges to start sending you information about their camps and questionnaires to complete during your sophomore year in high school. Starting September 1st of your junior year, schools can send you any recruiting material. You will get media guides, postcards, letters, notes, and relentless propaganda promoting the merits of various institutions. You will love going to the mailbox each day and seeing who cared enough to send you something today. The mail is one the best parts of recruiting.

Did you ever wonder how they found out about you? When you get mail from an in-state school you might think they read about you in the paper or heard about you on the radio or television, so now they are sending you a letter, and that happens. How did the out of state schools find out about me then? Has the word of your skills gone nationwide? Well, not quite.

Colleges get recommendations from a variety of sources. Their primary source is high school coaches. The college will send a questionnaire to your high school coach that asks them to recommend the top players on their team and in the area. A typical form will give some information about the college, like their academic requirements, so the coach knows what players could possibly get admitted. The coach will also decide who can play at the level of the school asking for the recommendation. If an offensive lineman is 5'10" and weighs 220 lbs he will probably not get recommended to go to Penn State. Coaches have to be prudent in their recommendations. If a high school coach gains a reputation as a guy who recommends all of his seniors to every D-I school every year, he will find it very hard to get a player recruited when he does have someone that could play at that level. It's kind of like the children's story of the man who cried wolf one too many times.

A sample of one of these recommendation forms sent to a high school coach is on the next page. This one is from Harvard University, it's old but it hasn't changed. The form asks the coach to recommend players that meet the criterion for admission. Notice on this form the first three are academic, and the fourth one is football ability. That is football in the Ivy League.

Also notice that it asks the high school coach to rate that player's football ability. Sometimes a high school coach will recommend a player to a school and not give him as high of a rating as possible. I have always made it a practice to rate my guys as high as I could. It never made sense to me why some coaches would recommend a player and then give him a low rating. Why did they bother to recommend him if they didn't think he could play at that level?

These forms typically ask the coach to recommend any younger players too. This gives those sophomores that have played a significant amount in varsity games and have potential, an opportunity get recommended and be in the college's database early. In addition they will ask for any players in the area but not at the school.

Harvard University

Tim Murphy
Head Coach

Dear Coach:

The Harvard football staff would greatly appreciate your cooperation in completing the attached prospect information card. We would like your advice and recommendation on student athletes who will be seniors next fall that you feel have the following qualifications:

1. Rank in the top 10% of their class
2. In strong Academic Program
3. Potential to score on the SAT (Verbal 600, Math 600, Writing 600)
4. Ability to play Division I/IAA football

We understand the busy schedule of coaches and the number of such inquiries you receive and thank you for any consideration you can give this request.

Best Regards,

Tim Murphy
Head Football Coach
Murr Center Football Office
Harvard University - Athletic Dept.
65 North Harvard Street
Boston, MA 02163

Harvard University Football

School: _____ Address: _____

City: _____ State: _____ Zip: _____

Head Coach: _____ Email: _____

Cell #: _____ Office #: _____ Home #: _____

Reverse Fold and Tape to Return — Please Print

Major College Football Rating Key: 1 - Rare Ability; 2 - Outstanding; 3 - Above Avg.; 4 - Avg.; 5 - Below Avg.

Prospect: _____ Position Offense: _____ Defense: _____ Rating: _____

Address: _____ City: _____ State _____ Zip: _____

Telephone: _____ Cell: _____ Email: _____

GPA: _____ Class Rank: _____ (P)Sat V _____ M: _____ W: _____ ACT: _____

HT _____ WT: _____ Jersey # _____ 40 Yard Time _____ 100M _____

Prospect: _____ Position Offense: _____ Defense: _____ Rating: _____

Address: _____ City: _____ State: _____ Zip: _____

Telephone: _____ Cell: _____ Email: _____

GPA _____ Class Rank: _____ (P)Sat V _____ M: _____ W: _____ ACT: _____

HT: _____ WT: _____ Jersey # _____ 40 Yard Time _____ 100M _____

Prospects in Your Area

Name: _____ Pos: _____ School: _____

Name: _____ Pos: _____ School: _____

Name: _____ Pos: _____ School: _____

Underclassmen Prospects at Your School

Name _____ Pos _____ School: _____

Name _____ Pos _____ School: _____

In addition to coaching recommendations, colleges will also use other sources to build their databases. With the emergence of internet companies like ESPN, Rivals100.com, Scout.com, Superprep.com and others, colleges closely monitor these sites to find players. Everybody is looking for that "diamond in the rough" guy that nobody knows about. Super Bowl MVP and All-Pro quarterback Tom Brady was one of those players. His dad made a videotape of him prior to his senior year and sent it to Michigan. After watching the tape the Wolverines contacted him and the rest is history. As the internet and recruiting services continue to expand their coverage of college recruiting, it will become harder and harder for coaches to find the guys that everybody misses.

Most recruiting is done regionally. However, you will get mail from everywhere. You will get mail from some schools that you will never talk to. When I was getting recruited the mail came from schools on the East Coast, the West Coast, and everywhere in between. Some of the schools that sent me the most mail I never heard from. I would get a letter several times a week from the University of Wyoming, but I never talked to any coach from that school. I always wondered why they sent me mail and never contacted me. Why would they waste all that money on postage? I imagine they got my name on their mailing list and never bothered to take it off. So what does it mean when you get a letter from a school?

Getting mail is better than not getting mail, but that is about it. Getting mail means the school knows about you. Getting mail means they might contact you. Getting mail does not mean a scholarship offer will follow. Schools with larger recruiting budgets have as many as 500 prospects on their mailing list. Most schools will sign anywhere from 20-25 kids a year so a lot of athletes get letters, and that's all. However, getting mail is better than not getting mail.

As you start to receive more and more mail you will start to get some questionnaires in some of those letters that schools want you to complete and return. The first couple you complete are exciting. However, as the questionnaires start to pile up you will become less and less excited about filling them out. I encourage you to persevere. Remember that every one you complete has the potential to turn into a scholarship. Look at each one as a job application and you are completing them for the best college job there is, to be a student-athlete.

However it brings up an interesting question, how do you view the recruiting process? Many athletes go into this thinking they are going have their egos stroked and their butts kissed. Coaches are going to beg them to come to their schools. I remember reading an article in Sports Illustrated about wide receiver Andre Hastings' list of demands for potential colleges. He insisted on having jersey #1, he would not red-shirt his freshman year, etc… As a high school student I thought recruiting was like that for everyone. In reality, it's only like that for about the top 5% of potential student athletes, for the rest of us, we are just looking for work. If this is your approach going in, 95% of you are going to be disappointed. Instead, I encourage you to look at the process like a job interview. You are getting ready to get out of high school and trying to find a way to get through college without the burden of having to pay back student loans in the end. You are looking for a job. If you do that, it changes your whole perspective on this process.

If you choose to look at this process like a job interview, one thing you are going to need is a resume. This will help to highlight your strengths and present you to potential employers, coaches, in a positive way. It shows that you care about this process, you take it very seriously, and you have a level of organization that will prepare you to be successful in college. In addition, rather than filling out all those questionnaires and repeatedly putting down some of the same information over and over, you can write a short cover letter and staple it to the questionnaire and return it with your resume. This way you get every one of them back quickly and increase your opportunities to get a job in the college football market.

A very common question I've received from student athletes over the years is, "What if I get a questionnaire from a school that I know I don't want to go to?" My standard answer is this, "If they were the only one to offer you a scholarship and it came down to them and having to pay to go to school, would you mind having a degree from their school hang on your wall?" For me the answer is simple, I wouldn't mind at all. We all are in different financial situations. Some can afford college, some cannot. Some parents started saving for college the day you were born, some could not. Some of you are willing to gamble and walk on and take a shot at earning a scholarship somewhere down the road at your dream school. I was not. I wanted the money up front and I would have gone anywhere that wanted me. It's like the Stephen Stills song goes, "If you can be with the one you love, honey, love the one you're with."

Along those same lines, a lot of questionnaires will also ask you to rate your interest in their school or rank the schools you are interested in attending. I would remind you at this point that everyone has an ego and nobody needs to be reminded they are not coaching the defending National Champions. When I was going through this I remember getting a letter from Iowa State. It asked me to list, in order, the schools I wanted to attend. Being a less than intelligent person, here was my list to Iowa State:

1. University of Iowa
2. Notre Dame
3. University of Michigan
4. University of Nebraska
5. Iowa State

Not exactly the best way to make friends and influence people. I would imagine the assistant coach that opened that survey when it returned was less than impressed by being ranked #5 and I am sure I dropped on his list too. It's kind of like writing Coca-Cola for a job and telling them you like Pepsi, Mountain Dew, Dr. Pepper, and Sprite all better, but if there is nothing else left you will choke down a Coke if you have to. Probably not the best approach.

It also reminds me of the questionnaire from the University of Missouri that asked me to rate my interest in their school on the following scale.

Strong   Very Interested   Average   Below Average   None

I could never figure out why when I put "Below Average" they stopped sending me letters. They must not have heard what a good player I was and didn't have the passion to recruit me, quitters. Or maybe there is a limited amount of resources every school has and if a player is not interested they put their money where players are interested.

Don't make the same mistakes I made. Create as many opportunities for yourself as you can by returning every survey, ranking the school that bought the stamp as high as possible, ranking your interest as high as possible, and remembering that it's a long way to signing day and you never know what school will be your new favorite. I joke with my players now that they should learn the following line, "I have dreamed my whole life of being a _____ (insert mascot name here)." Not a bad idea.

Joe Sample #1
Class of 2015

Address: 1234 Touchdown Road
Des Moines, IA 50311

Phone Number: (515) 555-5555

Parent/Guardian Names:
Paul & Kris Sample

Head Coach: Joe Hornback
Roosevelt High School
4419 Center Street
Des Moines, IA 50312-2299
School: (515) 242-7338
Home: (515) 277-2316
joseph.hornback@dmps.k12.ia.us

Top 2014 Games:
1.   Roosevelt vs. Hoover
2.   Roosevelt vs. East

j

Height: 5'10"
40 Time: 4.55

Weight: 180
Bench: 325

Position: Running Back
Squat: 370 **Power Clean:** 200

2014 Honors: 1st Team All-Conference, 2nd Team All League
Sophomore Season 1027 Yards Rushing, 14 Touchdowns. Team MVP.
2013 Honors: 1st Team All-Conference, 1st Team All-State,
Junior Season   Prep of the Week, Regular Season 4A Rushing Leader, 1st Team
All CIML.com web site, Team Captain, Team MVP. Holds
CIML Conference Records for Yards in a Game (333 Yards vs.
Hoover), Yards in a Season (1820 Yards in 2001), Attempts in a
Season (290 in 2001), and Touchdowns in a Season (22 in 2001).
In Track, Drake Relay Qualifier in the 4 x 100, 4 x 200, 4 x 400.
Ran a 11.03 second 100-yard dash. In wrestling, received the
Ironman Award.

2014 Honors: 1st Team All-Conference. 7 TD's against Hoover Broke Single Game
Record.
Senior Season   Roosevelt's All-Time Leading Rusher with 4361 yards! Voted MVP.

2013 Statistics   ***2014 Picture:***
1827 yards Rushing
290 Rushing Attempts
6.28 *Yards per Carry Average*
3 Receptions for 28 Yards
22 Touchdowns

2014 Statistics
1514 yards Rushing
192 Rushing Attempts
7.89 *Yards per Carry Average*
17 Receptions for 129 Yards
22 Touchdowns

Four Semester GPA: 4.0 /4.0
Class Rank: 1/376
Intended Area of Study: **Education**
ACT: 36

Chapter 3
Spring Evaluations

The first Thursday in February of your junior year is when recruiting really starts. Your senior friends will have signed their Letter of Intent the day before and now it's your turn. Colleges will shift their focus in a hurry and as soon as one class is wrapped up, they will start on the next one. Recruiting waits for no man.

As you are starting to get more and more mail you will notice that college coaches will be back in your high school. This is called the Spring Evaluation Period, from April 15th to May 31st. You will start to see college coaches at your track meets, baseball games, and if you live in a state that has spring football, at your spring football practices. They are starting the process of recruiting all over with a new group of players and they are there to see you.

During this period of time the college coaches are not allowed to schedule a meeting with you to market their school. They are allowed to come into your school, meet with your high school coaches, get film, get information, watch a track meet or baseball game, and then leave. If by chance they "bump" into a potential prospect they are allowed to say hello, but that is it. You would be amazed at the frequency that D-I coaches "bump" into D-I prospects every spring. In nine years as a head football coach, and 11 years as a principal, I helped a lot of coaches "bump" into a lot of players.

As a player that is treating the recruiting process as a job interview I have five pointers to help you through this period.

#1. Be in class.

As silly as this one sounds, you would be amazed how hard it is to find a moving target. I've had players over the years that were hard to "bump" into because I could not find them. One spring I looked up a player's class schedule after meeting with a coach to learn that he was in math class. As the college coach and I are walking up to the class I found myself saying things like:

"He really loves math. You should see him do long division."

"Math and this young man is like a duck in water, it just looks right."

"He is one heck of a mathlete in addition to being a fabulous athlete."

And on and on I went. It was slightly embarrassing when I knocked on the classroom door and invited myself in to find the young man was not in class and the math teacher said with a chuckle, "Oh him, he is never here."

Undeterred, the search continued. I had seen the young man in the library a few times so I took a shot at finding him there. As we walked, I found myself saying things like:

"He loves to read, you can't get him out of here."

"One of his hobbies is reading to the children, he is such a giver."

"Read, read, read, that is all this kid does."

As we walked in the library and realized he was nowhere to be found, I started to become concerned. However, I was not ready to give up just yet. As we walked to the cafeteria I may have started to sound less convincing as I told the coach:

"He usually gets a snack at this time because he is always giving his lunch away."

"The lunch ladies always need help moving big things down here, I bet that is what he is doing."

"He may have just needed some space to stretch out and do his math, you should see how big these tables are."

Needless to say he was not in there either. I later learned that he had been sitting out on a park bench sleeping or something equally important. This obviously an exaggeration, but it illustrates the importance of being where you should be, it is much easier to find a guy to accidentally "bump" into if he is where he is supposed to be, when he is supposed to be there.

#2. Wear nice clothes.

It amazes me what some guys wear to school. Some players roll out of bed, put on a pair of shorts and come to school. No shower, no deodorant, no brushing of the teeth, nothing. They sleep as late as they possibly can, then they fall out of bed and rush to school.

You wouldn't think twice about going to a job interview without wearing a collared shirt, pants, belt, and shoes. It should be just as easy to make that same choice during your junior year in March and April. You are going to meet coaches that will determine if you get recruited. They will not base their decision entirely on what you wear to school of course, but it never hurts to try to make a good impression the first time you meet.

#3. Carry a book.

One of my duties as a high school teacher was to monitor the halls during passing period. I was always amazed at the number of students that walk down the hall fat, dumb, and happy and not a care in the world. No books, no paper, no pen, no plan at all. They are just happy to be there and oblivious to what they are in school to do, to learn. They are there to talk to the ladies, hang out with their friends, eat lunch, and when they are not doing that they will sit in a room and watch a teacher work. They are not there to learn. They are along for the ride and they will do just enough to get by and graduate while learning as little as they can, doing the minimum, and no more. Don't be this guy.

Be a student first, then an athlete. Be a serious student first who cares about what he learns first, and about his grades second. Be someone who is not mistaken for stereotypical jock who is in school just so he can play in the games and relies on his reputation to keep him eligible. As one of the top athletes in your class you are a leader in more ways than one. If you take that responsibility seriously then you will find it easier to be a leader in the classroom too.

When you bump into that college coach in the spring and you are carrying a chemistry book, or pre-calculus book, or something like that, it sends a big message to that coach that you are a serious student. You are someone who cares about school. You show that you are someone who will have no trouble getting into college and passing the NCAA requirements. You send a positive message that you are not going to be someone that he is going to have to baby-sit for four years to make sure you are going to class and will be eligible each semester and will graduate at the end. Show that coach the first time you meet him that you are a student first and someone who will take care of business in the classroom in college because you did it in high school.

#4. Stand up straight.

A car salesman once told me the two biggest lies that men tell is how much they paid for their house, and how much they paid for their last car. Men will exaggerate how much their house cost to make themselves sound wealthy, and minimize what they paid for their last car to make them sound like they are good negotiators. The biggest lie told in recruiting is how tall you are. If you are 5'10" coaches usually round that up to 6 feet. Everyone over 6' we usually add an inch or two to make them sound like a better prospect. Somehow an offensive lineman sounds better if he is 6'4" instead of 6'2". A defensive back sounds like he can play in college better if he is 6' and not 5'10". College coaches know that high school coaches usually add an inch or two and this is the reason so many want to "bump" into the prospect to see how much we lied this year.

As a result, stand up as tall as you can when you meet these coaches. If you are 6'4", then be 6'4". Don't slouch and be 5'11". You will notice that when a lot of these coaches meet you they will shake hands and then pull you close to them and stand as close to you as possible. This is not because they are trying to smell you or anything weird like that, they are trying to get a feel for how tall you are. Your high school coach just told him you were 6'4", now he wants to see for himself.

#5. Thank the coach.

Gratitude never goes out of style and everyone likes to be thanked. When you meet that college coach for the first time and he shakes your hand say something like, "Coach, thank you for coming to my high school today and talking to my coach about me. I really appreciate it." Wow. What an impression you would make then. Remember there are a lot of other players out there and he took the time to come to your school and meet with your coach and wanted to bump into you, the very least you can do is to thank him.

Guess what happens when we walk to your class to bump into you and you are sitting there with a book open, actively participating, wearing nice clothes, and you excuse yourself to come out into the hall to meet the coach. You stand up tall and shake his hand, look him in the eye and thank him for taking the time to come to your school and talk to you and your coach. When you go back into the room and your high school coach walks back down the hall with the college coach, guess what the college coach says nine out of ten times? "Nice kid." You made an impression that you may be someone he could see coaching for the next five years.

He came to the school to see what he cannot see on film, can't tell from your survey that you filled out, or what your high school coach wouldn't tell him. He came to get an impression of you. If the high school visit was not important, he could have sat in his office on his campus and done other things to get ready for next season, but he chose to come to your school on that day to see what you were like. Make sure you send him away with the true picture of who you are.

Chapter 4
Phone Calls

The NCAA regulates the number of times colleges can call. It was not always that way. I can remember walking into the coaches' office at the University of Kansas when I was a freshman and reading the sign above the door that said, "Recruiting Is Like Shaving: If You Miss A Day You Look Like Crap." It used to be common for coaches to call several times a week, on holidays, late at night, etc... The thinking was that if coaches didn't call every day, other coaches would, and they would miss out on some players.   No coach wants to be outworked and most college coaches have a Type-A personality so many of them would call their top guys all the time. Thankfully, the NCAA imposed some rules for the colleges to enable the high school athlete to enjoy his high school experience more. According to NCAA rules colleges are allowed to call one time in the May of an athlete's junior year, and then they cannot call again until September of their senior year. Then coaches are allowed to call an athlete once a week.

When coaches call, give them your full attention. An assistant coach from an SEC school told me the following story. He was making his recruiting calls one night in the fall after practice. The staff he was on had a meeting start that morning at 7:00 a.m. and last until noon. Then he watched film after lunch to get ready for his practice that day. He did a radio interview, wrote his practice schedule and meeting plan, went to practice, training table and then back to the office to watch the video of practice and work some more. He was calling recruits on the west coast to take advantage of the time difference. It was 11:30 p.m. for him on the East Coast, but only 8:30 p.m. for the athlete on the West Coast. It had been over a 16 hour day so far and he had one more call to make. The young man he was talking to was not much of a phone talker. The coach would ask questions and the player would mumble one or two word answers. In addition, he could hear the PlayStation game and the recruit's buddies in the background asking him to get off the phone while giving him a hard time. The coach closed his eyes as he was talking to the recruit, each answer took longer and longer to get. The next thing he heard was laughter on the other end of the phone. The coach had fallen asleep and started to snore. The recruit passed the phone around the room so his friends could hear the coach sawing logs. He woke up as they burst into laughter.

The coach was obviously embarrassed, but he is not all to blame. At the end of a long day and talking to a recruit who was not giving him much attention, it's reasonable to see how he dosed off. The recruit didn't understand either the significance of what was happening. He did not fully appreciate the fact that this coach could pay his way through college. That conversation could be worth $150,000! Is $150,000 worth your time? When your friends are paying back their student loans, you could spend that money on other things. When that coach calls, turn off the television, press pause on the game you are playing, walk in the other room away from your friends, and spend time with the coach calling. Furthermore, in the fall as you start to talk to coaches more and more, schedule a time to talk. If you know you have church on Wednesday nights and your game is on Friday, ask coaches to call on Tuesdays and Thursdays from 6:00 p.m. to 8:00 p.m. During that time, give them your full attention. Invest your time in getting to know these coaches and more importantly let them get to know you. I am always surprised how many boisterous young men get shy around a new adult. Guys who are loud and obnoxious in the locker room will become meek and passive when they meet someone new. Relax, be yourself. Be someone the coaches want to spend five years with. Remember they are calling because they want you to come to their school so be confident and allow them to get to know you. Sometimes that is hard to do, so here is something to think about.

I have been hired to be a head football coach twice. In both interviews I sat in front of a committee of people and answered a list of questions they asked all the other candidates. It is common when you have multiple candidates for the same job to ask them the same list of questions. In science we call these fixed variables. The independent variable is the person answering the questions; the fixed variables are the questions themselves. In your process to evaluate colleges I would encourage you to take the same approach. The colleges will be different, but you should ask the same questions to each so it's easier to compare them. In addition, if you have a list of questions that you can ask any coach that calls then if you get nervous and don't know what to say, you already have your conversation planned out in advance. It's kind of like when you are calling a girl you really like for the first time, you have an idea before you dial the number what you want to talk about so you make a good impression. Treat these coaches like that pretty girl you want to impress.

Enclosed is a sample form you can use when coaches call, but I encourage you to add and delete some of these questions based on what you want to know. As you are talking to the coach, take some notes about your conversation. This will help you stay engaged and it will help produce a productive conversation. Furthermore, you will be amazed at how you can ask five coaches the same question and get five different answers. One of my favorite questions to ask coaches as I meet them in recruiting is, "What is the best part of your football program?" I get answers that range from their tradition to their academic support staff. New staffs that are taking over bad programs talk about the future. Teams that have been successful talk about their success. Everyone talks about their commitment to helping student-athletes be successful in the classroom. You can really get a sense of what is important to the coaches when you ask that question.

If I was a player getting ready to start this process, knowing what I know now, I would ask the question, "What is your coaching style?" If I go there am I going to be a number, a piece of meat, or do you get to know your players? What are some things you do that support what you say your coaching philosophy is? If you say that it's important to develop relationships with players, then what activities do you do to help accomplish that goal? I had a great college football experience, but there is a reason I am a high school football coach. I enjoy the relationship part of coaching the most and my passion is helping young men become good men. Unfortunately, that is not the focus of a lot of college football programs. The focus is on winning, and winning right now. Every coach wants to win, that is what makes us competitive, but I would want to know if the coach was interested in helping me develop as a person too.

Every coach is going to care about you as a player, I would want to know who is going to care about me as a person. Remember this process is about finding the right fit for both you and the college, don't be afraid to ask a lot of questions to the coaches. As I am sure you have heard many times in school, "The only bad question is the one you don't ask."

College: _____

Coach's Name: _____

Position he Coaches: _____

Phone Number: _____

email: _____

Date   Subjects Discussed

_____

_____

_____

_____

Questions to Ask:

1.   What is the best part of your football program?

_____

_____

2.   What are your players doing now?

_____

_____

3.   What are your prospects for this season?

_____

_____

4.   What position do you think I will play at your school?

_____

_____

5. Do you offer the academic area I am interested in studying?

_____

_____

6. What is your program's coaching style?

_____

_____

7. What type of offense/defense do you run?

_____

_____

8. What type of academic support does your school offer student-athletes?

_____

_____

9. What is your graduation rate?

_____

_____

10. What happens to me if I get injured while I am playing at your school?

_____

_____

11. Where would I live if I went to your school?

_____

_____

12. What do most of the guys on the team do in the summer?

_____

_____

13. Are there any employment opportunities available for student-athletes?

_____

_____

14. What is a typical day like for a student-athlete during the season?

_____

_____

15. What is a typical day like for a student-athlete during the off-season?

_____

_____

** Thank him for calling!
** Ask him if he has tape. Check with high school coach to see if tape has been sent or shared!

The NCAA rules about phone contact only apply to the colleges. You can call all you want. If you have questions, call the coach. Most schools now have an 1-800 number you can call so its toll free for you. However, most people have cell phones that do not distinguish between local and long distance calls so the toll free numbers are less important.

Remember that the coaches are restricted in the number of times they can call you so if you call to ask a question and leave a voicemail, do not be discouraged if the coach does not call you back. It could be that he cannot do it. For example, coaches are not allowed to call players in June, July, or August before a recruit's senior year. They can call once in May, but then not again until September. You decide you want to take a visit to the school to see campus and meet the coaches over the summer. In July, you call the coach you talked to in May and leave a message for him. He does not call you back and you think it's because the school is no longer interest in recruiting you, but that may not be the case. He can't call you back. Many coaches put this on their greeting when you get their voicemail or the secretary who answers the phone may remind you of this when you call. Remember the rules of contact only apply to them and not you. I say this to my players every year and invariably I will have an athlete walk into the weight room one day in July and be very discouraged. When I ask him what is going one he says, "No coaches are calling me. I don't think I am going to get recruited." I scratch my head and remind them of the rule.

Electronic communication between coaches and players are currently not regulated by the NCAA, primarily email and faxing. If you have access to email and have an email address coaches will send out email on regular basis. A lot of the email you will get will be similar to the bulk mail you get in recruiting. It will be information about the school or upcoming events in football or their athletic programs. Some mail will be personalized and will require a response. Like all your snail mail with return envelopes, you want to make sure you respond to the emails that want a response.

Text messaging was the next big thing in recruiting. If you had a cell phone and could receive text messages, coaches would send text messages by the dozen. However, the NCAA started to get complaints from parents about the number of messages players would receive, and the bills the parents would get who didn't have cell phone plans with unlimited texting. As a result, in 2007 they changed the rule and college football coaches were not allowed to send text messages to players. They can still do it in basketball, but football coaches could not.

Social media has probably influenced recruiting as much as anything in last ten years. Rather than relying on text messaging, email, or faxing, coaches will direct message athletes on Twitter, friend them on Facebook, follow them on Instagram, or find another way to communicate with athletes that is not regulated by the NCAA. Coaches have included social media research in their recruiting process to research potential student activities and monitor their recruiting process. This creates a unique opportunity and a challenge at the same time. Each athlete can market themselves in a positive way, or they can jeopardize their recruiting by posting inappropriate pictures and comments. I would encourage you to look at every posting like an interview with a reporter. If you would be comfortable with a reporter including your comments or pictures in a story they are writing about you for the newspaper, then go ahead and post it on the internet. If not, the delete button is your friend.

Chapter 5
Unofficial Visits

The difference between an unofficial and an official visit is who pays the bill. On an unofficial visit the recruit will pay for all of his expenses associated with the trip. This includes his travel expenses, hotel, food, and other expenses associated with his visit, with the exception of game tickets which can be supplied. On an official visit, the school will pay for everything, however on this trip you have to pick up the check.

One spring I had several players invited to attend a basketball game at a school that was interested in recruiting them the following fall. Their parents had to work, and they didn't drive, so they asked me to take them to campus and spend the day. We called ahead of time and informed the school we would be attending, always a good idea, and headed off to campus on a Saturday morning. We arrived at the stadium and were shown a highlight film of the previous season and given a tour of the football facility. Following a campus tour we met back at the stadium and had an opportunity to talk to the coaches. They had sandwiches for the recruits before we left for the basketball game, but we had to pay $5 for them. One of the players with us commented, "These coaches are cheap. I can't believe we have to pay for this." He did not understand the concept of unofficial. We were given tickets to the game, but in order for it to be considered and unofficial visit we had to pay for our own lunch and gas to get to campus.

Some examples of unofficial visits include, but are not limited to: basketball games, junior days, spring football games, spring football practices, summer open houses, and fall football games. You are not limited to a certain number of unofficial visits and you should attend as many as your schedule and finances will allow. All of these are events you are invited to, but you can contact a school and set up your own unofficial visit.

Here are some tips for handling unofficial visits.

1. RSVP

Nobody likes surprises or uninvited guests. If you decide you want to go to an unofficial type event a school is having, call ahead of time and tell them you would like to attend. It's better if you are invited, but if you would like to come to an event you have not been invited to, call ahead and see if it's okay. Most of the time coaches will not have a problem with you coming unless they have a limited number of tickets to a basketball game or football game. College coaches love it when potential recruits want to come on campus because it gives them an opportunity to sell their program and it is not counted as one of their contacts. However, nobody likes it when someone crashes their junior day. It is not good for the school and definitely not good for the recruit.

If you would like to come on a day they are not having an event that is okay too, but you really should call ahead before you show up. This gives the school an opportunity to make sure someone is able to spend some time with you and it makes your visit much more productive. I coached a young man that had numerous D-I offers his senior year and he really took advantage of the unofficial visits. He and his father took ten days in the summer and got in the truck and drove around visiting five different schools. They called each school beforehand and set up their trip so each school could have a coach meet with them and show them around. Following this trip, the recruit had a very good idea of what school he wanted to attend because he took the time to visit when he had time, and he was able to make a good choice that fit his needs. By setting up the visits beforehand he was able to give the coaches an opportunity to be prepared when he arrived.

2. Put your "Cool Card" away.

Some guys refused to be impressed. I have seen kids walk into a 15 million dollar indoor facility and say, "This is alright." You have to be kidding me! Alright? Just alright? How can you not be impressed when you walk into that facility? I don't know what your high school is like, but all of the ones that I have attended and worked in have nothing like this!

Remember that football facilities serve two purposes; function and recruiting. They need that indoor facility so they have someplace to go when it's cold or raining, that is function. They want that indoor facility so when people like you come on campus you say, "Holy Cow! This is awesome!" When I first arrived at the University of Kansas the offensive line met in a closet that held track equipment. We had about fifteen chairs, each a different color, a big television on a cart, a dry erase board, and a collapsible metal fence with a chain and lock to keep the television from being stolen. In Kansas in August its about 15 degrees hotter than hell on a warm day, so when they showed us to our no air conditioned meeting facility I said to one of my classmates, "This was not on the tour." Thankfully they were in the process of building a new facility with updated locker rooms and big beautiful meeting rooms with air conditioning, matching chairs, mounted televisions from the ceiling, and carpet. We moved in there my sophomore year, it was like Christmas, it was 1993. In the winter of 2005, just 12 years later the University received a large gift from an alum for a new football facility. In an online article describing the gift it said that KU "needed" the facility because it had the worst facilities in the Big 12. They should have seen them before.

Don't be afraid to be impressed. Verbalize that you are impressed. Comment to coaches and hosts how impressed you are by the facilities. They build them for you, put your "cool card" away and allow yourself to show others around you that you are impressed.

3. Everyone has an ego and gratitude never goes out of style.

During the summer prior to my senior year my dad and I drove from Des Moines, Iowa to Ann Arbor, Michigan to see the university. We made an event out of it. We stopped in Detroit and watched the Tigers play baseball, we ate at local restaurants the entire time, the whole trip was a lot of fun. I loved Michigan as a kid. Their helmets and fiery coach, Bo Shembechler, made me want to be a Wolverine. My dad knew this and he wanted me to see the campus so he decided to take me on this trip. The university was having a junior day event and invited me to attend, along with a lot of other players. When we arrived I introduced myself to the coach who had been calling me (there was not a rule at the time that coaches could not call in the summer) and we checked in. I noticed right away that I was not like a lot of the other offensive lineman they had invited. I was barely 6'2" and it seemed like all the other offensive lineman towered over me. It amazed me how big some of those guys were. All through grade school, middle school, and high school I had always been the biggest kid in my class. It was clear that those days had come to an end. I started to get a little insecure and uncomfortable.

The coaches gave us a walking tour of the campus and football facilities. It was beautiful. We walked in their famous stadium, The Big House, and stood at the 50-yard line. The field was turf at the time and had a permanent "M" painted at midfield. I stood right on top of it and looked in all directions wondering what it would be like to play there. At the time I remember thinking that if Michigan did not offer me a scholarship, surely Iowa would, and I would be back there again some day. As it turned out, neither school did, and I have not been back since.

As we completed our walking tour of the campus we approached the parking lot where we had parked our car. The group was headed to the football facility, but it would be quicker to go straight to the car rather than stay with the group. It was a long drive home and I knew my dad wanted to get on the road. As the day had progressed I had overheard some of the other recruits talk about what coaches had contacted them, the other trips they had planned, and what scholarship offers they had already received. I was already a little intimidated by the size of some of these monsters, now I was more than a little jealous of the attention they were receiving from colleges. I was used to being the big fish in a small pond, so it was humbling to see that my pond now included a few whales. As a result, when the opportunity presented itself to sneak out a little early I did not hesitate.

I let my ego get in the way of the recruiting process. Looking back now, one of the things I wish I would have done was express my gratitude to the coach who invited me to the event. I should have taken the time to walk back to the football facility and find the coach and said, "Coach, thank you for inviting me to this event. I really enjoyed it. I look forward to talking to you more in the future." Would it have made a difference in them offering me a scholarship? I doubt it, but you never know. I had an opportunity to make a great impression, and I dropped the ball. I was more worried about my own bruised ego, and I forgot he had one too. Gratitude never goes out of style, so I wish now I would have taken the time to express mine.

When you go on one of these trips, remember that everyone has an ego and gratitude never goes out of style. Make sure you thank the coach for the tickets to the basketball game, the tour of campus, his time he spent with you. This is your opportunity to make a great impression. Be someone they want to spend the next five years coaching. Allow your personality to show, be confident, and above all, remember that even if you don't stack up physically to the competition in your eyes, you were invited too so the coaches must see something in you, even if you can't.

4. Be aware of what you wear and how you act.

I have heard this story several times from different coaches around the country. A school is having an unofficial visit event, such as a spring football game or junior day, and a potential recruit shows up wearing clothing promoting a rival school of the one hosting the junior day. I heard an LSU coach talk about a kid showing up wearing an Alabama sweatshirt, a Kansas coach talk about a recruit walking in with Missouri jersey on, and an Oklahoma coach tells a story of a young man coming in with a full Texas outfit: hat, jogging suit, t-shirt, the whole nine yards. These kids are either arrogant or ignorant.

They must think their skills are so good they can show up wearing the rival teams colors and coaches will not be offended. They have to be convinced the coaches want them so bad they can walk into their house and slap them in face and the college will come back begging for more. Have some sense; you don't go to a Coke interview wearing a Pepsi shirt. Why would you walk on a college campus as a guest of the athletic department, and promote another school.

The only other explanation is ignorance. You don't know this will bother the coaches who invited you, or you think it is funny. Either way, it is not the best way to make a good first impression. I had a speaking engagement one year in Hattiesburg, Mississippi and I talked about this topic in my speech and used the LSU coach and Alabama sweatshirt example. A mother came up to me afterwards and wanted to know exactly what the LSU coach had said to me. I talked to her for a few minutes and at the end I asked her why she was so interested and she said, "That was my older son that did that." She said she had told him not to wear that, but he did not think it was a big deal and thought his mother was overreacting. I asked her where her son played now, and she told me, "Arkansas State." I doubt her son was the only one to do it at LSU and he may not have been the one the coach was talking about, but I hear this story all the time around the country. Trust me on this, the college coach does not find it funny.

Chapter 6
Summer Camps

When you were a kid you may have gone to summer camp. You probably collected firewood, put up tents, went fishing, and made s'mores. You and your buddies looked forward to staying up late and looking at the stars. Summer camp was the best. The only thing you had to do before camp was to pack your backpack and make sure your sleeping bag was ready for another year. Those were the good old days. This summer you may go on a similar trip; however, it will <u>not</u> be at the college football camp you choose to attend.

When you go to camp this summer it is one thing and one thing only, a tryout. You will be invited to many camps and every college coach has the same agenda when they invite you, they want to see if you can play on their team. You are coming on campus so they can evaluate you in person. Your high school coach may have told the college coach about you, he may have seen you on video, now it's his chance to see you for himself.

When I was in high school I did not get it. I was invited to go to the University of Iowa camp prior to my senior season. They told me in the spring they were interested in signing one center, and I arrogantly assumed I was the only one they were recruiting. I went to camp about 25 pounds overweight and in terrible shape. I knew right away I had made a mistake.

The first thing we did at camp was to run a 40 yard dash. I was a typical offensive lineman that mocked the idea of having to run a 40. Most O-linemen are equipped with some version of the following line as a defense mechanism: "If I ever have to run 40 yards in a game something has gone terribly wrong." I didn't think it was important for me to be fast for 40 yards, unfortunately the University of Iowa did not agree. I lumbered up to the start line and shot out of a football stance and ran as hard as I could. When I finished, I jogged over to the O-line coach who had been watching and asked what my time was.

"5.47" he replied.

"Is that good?" I asked, already knowing the answer by his expression.

"If you are running backwards." He quipped.

"Why don't I run it again." I replied.

"That would be a good idea. Make sure you are really stretched out." He encouraged.

Again I approached the line and fired out of my football stance and labored for 40 grueling yards. Again I was slow.

"Was that better?" I asked cautiously.

"Yeah, that was a 5.45." he responded.

What I did not realize at the time leading up to camp was the Hawkeyes were not going to put all of their eggs in one basket. There was another guy there that day trying to get recruited too. His name was Casey Wiegmann. Casey ended up signing with Iowa, had a great college career and then was signed as undrafted free agent by the Chicago Bears and went on to play for the Kansas City Chiefs, spending over 10 years in the NFL. Casey was from a small school in Iowa and I was from one of the largest and best known high schools in the state. I thought I had an advantage, and I did until it was time to run. Camp really worked out for him.

Before you go to camp you should ask yourself the following question; will going to this camp increase my chances of getting a scholarship? Some guys pass the "eyeball test" with ease. When they walk down the street people look at them and say, "That guy looks like a big time football player." If you are one of those guys, and you run well too, then camp is the best thing for you. If you are an o-lineman who is 6'6" and can run around 5.0, no belly, and look athletic then you can go to camp and leave with a scholarship. The most important physical characteristic is height. Coaches' figure that weight can be improved with diet and training, but height is a deal breaker. If you are not tall enough for your position you are at a big disadvantage. I am not saying it does not happen, but it is an uphill battle.

Speed is a very close second to height. I once heard a track coach say, "Our athletes get faster with either B-F-S or G-O-D." BFS stands for the Bigger, Faster, Stronger training program, God is your genetics. Most coaches believe this too. They think they can help get you faster in college, but if you are slow now they can make you less slow, but never fast. If you run like I did, stay home, all you will do is take money off the table.

Now before I go any further let me make one thing clear, a D-I football player and a D-I athlete are not always the same person. On every team, in every league in America there is a guy making plays that has no business doing it. We call those guys, "Enough Guys" because they are just fast enough, just quick enough, just strong enough, just big enough etc… I remember my college coach Glen Mason used to say, "There are some guys that just make plays!" You hear about these guys all the time, they make great TV stories. These are the guys who really love the game, are smart, understand what it takes and they just make plays. They are not impressive walking out of the locker room, but from snap to whistle they can flat out play football. There are guys on your favorite college team right now just like this. There are a lot of guys playing in the NFL like this too. Every year more talented, faster, more athletic guys come out of college and try to take their jobs, but the veteran who understands the game and plays with great technique keeps his job year after year. How does he do it, simple, he can play football. And for all this talk about how important your height and speed are in recruiting the most important thing is whether or not you can play the game. Coaches will use these as indicators for prospects, but they are looking for guys who can play.

So ask yourself the question, "Will going to this camp increase my chances of getting a scholarship?" If you pass the "eyeball test" and run well then go and knock their socks off and leave camp with a scholarship offer. If the answer is no, then you should not go and hope your film is good enough to get you recruited. It is a gamble, but if you are good enough to play there, they will see it on film.

Before you go to any camps, I encourage you to include your high school coach in the process. If you decide you want to go to a camp, ask your high school coach call the college coach and ask the following question, "Are you planning to recruit Johnny to play at your school?" High school coaches develop relationships with college coaches because we talk to them every year. A college coach can only say one of three things to that question; yes, no, or we are not sure.

If the college coach says "yes, we are going to offer him" then what do you gain by going to camp? If your goal is to get a scholarship, and they have already offered you one, if you don't do well at camp they can take it back. You have not signed a letter of intent, it is non-binding on both sides, if they don't like what they see they can rescind the offer. You will either go and validate their feelings about you or you could cause them to change their mind about you. I think it's a no win deal. At best it is a tie-lose deal.

If the college coach says "no, he does not fit our plans" then why in the world would you go to that camp? These camps are expensive and your goal is to get a scholarship offer. If the school has already said "no", save your time and money and invest it in something with some possibilities.

If the college says, "we don't know, we need to see him in person" then you have to go back to the previous question: "Will going to this camp increase my chances of getting a scholarship offer?" If you think you can go in and test well and you look the part, create an opportunity for yourself. If you don't fall into that category, then beg off and make so many plays your senior year on tape and force them to recruit you. I use this term a lot with my players. Force them to recruit you because you make so many plays the alumni of the school would go berserk if they did not offer you a scholarship. Force them to look at the tape and say they can't live without you. Force them to look at the tape and recruit you because they don't want you playing for their rival and have to scheme against you for the next four years. If you don't pass they "eyeball test" or if your 40 time will not wow them, then go old school and score touchdowns, make tackles, intercept passes, dominate the line of scrimmage, throw touchdowns, manage the game, out hustle, out care, and out play everyone on the field. Force them to look at your tape and say, "That guy just makes plays and we have to have him!"

College football camps are an audition, a tryout, and an interview all wrapped in one. If you decide to go make sure you understand that, and you are in the best shape of your life. It is a business trip so leave your PS 2 at home and make sure you get plenty of rest and fluids while you are there. Be the first in line to every drill and make sure you stand out. They are not looking for the average camper; they are looking for the guys that are head and shoulders better than everyone else there. Don't go and be average, average guys don't get recruited, if you go, you had better be exceptional!

Chapter 7
Frequently Asked Questions

In this chapter I am going to divide the Frequently Asked Questions into two categories. *Frequently Asked Questions by Parents* and *Frequently Asked Questions by College Coaches*. From 2000 to 2010 I was the featured speaker for over Junior Days for Rivals100.com, Yahoo!, and FBU (Football University) events. Over those 10 years I gave approximately 75 presentations on the recruiting process to prospective student athletes and answered questions. After each presentation, there were some questions I got asked after every speech. I tried to modify my speech to hit these topics, but some are not easy to talk about to the entire group so I deal with them in a one on one manner.

The other category, *Frequently Asked Questions by College Coaches*, are a summary of what high school coaches and college coaches talk about. My players would ask me all the time, "What do you and the college coach talk about for so long in your office?" The answer is simple, you.

Frequently Asked Questions by Parents:
   1. **What do I do if my son is not being recruited?**
   It depends on why your son is not being recruited. If he is not a good enough player, a hard pill for some parents to swallow, then there is not much that can be done except to lower your expectations. A lot of kids get caught up in the mentality of D-I or bust and they don't even want to

consider going to a D-IAA or D-II school because their pride will not allow it. In my mind a scholarship is a scholarship and a degree from a D-II school will still get you a job and leave you debt free or with low debt.

If your son is not getting recruited because he is not getting promoted by his high school coach, that is an easier one to fix. Remember in Chapter 2 when we talked about recruiting mail and making a recruiting resume? If you have a resume prepared and take it to your high school head coach and say, "Coach, I would really like to go to _____ University and I have not heard anything from them. Would you mind sending this on my behalf and contacting them for me?" Sometimes that's all it takes. He makes a phone call or sends an email, forwards your resume and now you are on their radar. Always work through the recruiting coordinator of the college you would like to attend. He is the gatekeeper that starts the process going for you with each school. You still have to be good enough to play there, but that should get the ball rolling.

2. What if my high school coach will not help my son?

Unfortunately, I get this question a lot. Sometimes there is personality conflict with a coach or a coach has resigned and does not feel it's his responsibility since he is no longer the coach. Either scenario is not positive. If you meet with the high school coach and he will not help you, then you should take the next step. The most important thing is the player gets promoted so I recommend you talk to your athletic director or principal and see what can be done. The athletic director or principal can do the same thing the coach can as far as contacting the college coaches on your behalf and start the process for you. The college coach is still going to contact the high school coach to see why he is being contacted by the AD or principal, so there is no way to cut him out of the process completely. Hopefully, he will be a professional and speak honestly about the player.

As a last resort you can contact the school yourself, but I would only do this as an absolute last possible option. When college coaches get things from parents it is always viewed with great skepticism. The first question they have is, "Why didn't the coach send me this if the kid is that good?" However, it is better than not getting promoted at all.

3.   Should we hire a recruiting service to promote our son?

A good high school coach beats a recruiting service any day. I have heard these guys give their sales pitch to parents about how they are investing in their son's future by hiring their company to promote their son. They justify their price by saying things like, "Is a $1500 investment now worth it to get a scholarship?" The problem is they cannot guarantee you are going to get a scholarship. I always wanted to say to one of them,

"Will you refund me the money if it doesn't work out?" I doubt they would.

To understand recruiting you have to understand two very important principles: the high school coach is critical and most recruiting is done regionally. Scouting service talk about how they will promote your son from coast to coast. The problem is that most schools do not have the budget to recruit nationwide. Most schools stay within the states surrounding their state to find players. The only real exception is that everyone recruits Texas. So if you live in the state of Washington and somebody from a recruiting service promises you will get recruited by East Coast schools, he is probably speaking out of turn. Most schools on the coasts are not going to pay airfare for their assistants to travel back and forth several times a year to find players. In addition, schools are trying to sell season tickets and more people buy tickets when they have a player on the college team that they followed in high school. Most college coaches are not successful if they don't close the borders and get the best players in their state; it is bad practice and terrible public relations when the top high school players in their state go somewhere else to play in college.

Second, very few guys get scholarship offers without the college coach at least talking to the high school coach. Unless the player is a slam dunk prospect the high school coach is usually talked to about the potential recruit. If you leave the high school coach out of the equation, you are just going to have to catch him up later on in the process what has happened.

As you can probably tell I am not a big fan of these services. My experience is that a lot of times they include empty promises and they don't deliver as often as they would like. If you know someone that has gone through recruiting and they had a good experience with one and felt like they did what they said they would do, and your high school coach is not a big fan of recruiting, then maybe you should hire one. If you do decide to do it, ask for a list of their previous clients and see how they did for them. Don't just use there references, talk to the people they don't want you to talk to and find out if you are really going to get what they promised.

4. **How do you get noticed by Rivals.com, Scout.com, and other recruiting websites?**

More than any other media source, the internet has changed recruiting the most since 1991 when I signed my letter of intent. Alumni now buy subscriptions to websites so they can track the recruiting of their school. Fans now go online to check out how many stars a recruiting website gave a prospect their school just signed. It has become big business. High school players want to be recognized by these sites and ranked high for their egos and to increase their marketability to schools. College coaches monitor these sites daily to make sure their databases are up to date with the prospects in their recruiting region. The internet has helped more high school players get recognized so fewer guys slip through the cracks.

However, what do you do if you are not in the websites database? The same thing you should do if you are not being recruited by a college. Ask your coach to contact the editor of the website and recommend you. Most sites have an online recommendation form that coaches, players, and parents can complete. Again I would recommend letting your coach do it, because it will be viewed as an objective recommendation rather than one coming from a parent. However, if your coach is not computer literate, then go ahead and recommend yourself, send in some tape and make sure you are on these databases. Colleges look at them everyday so make sure they see you there.

5. **How are IVY League schools different from other NCAA schools?**

In Chapter 8, the Clearinghouse, I go into detail about what the academic requirements are in order for a high school senior to become eligible for an NCAA institution. Those are NCAA guidelines, they are not national guidelines. Colleges have the right to make their admission standards higher than NCAA minimum eligibility standards, and most do. The IVY League standards are much higher than the NCAA standards. You don't see anybody at Harvard that graduated with a 2.5 GPA and had a 18 on his ACT, I don't care how well they play football.

However, football can help you get into an IVY League school. They call it, "supporting your application." It means that if you are a candidate for an IVY League school and a good football player, the football coach can be an advocate for your admission. Once the coach has evaluated your athletic ability and academic standing, he will encourage you to apply to the school. Once your application is complete, he will take it from there. If you are a strong candidate then he can help make the difference in whether or not you are admitted. When talking to an IVY League coach, ask him if he will support your application, he will know what you are talking about.

Frequently Asked Questions by College Coaches

As a head football coach for a number of years I have talked to hundreds of college coaches about hundreds of high school players. There are some questions that come up in every conversation. As you read this section, think about how your high school coach would answer this question about you. Not how you would want him to answer, not how you think he should answer, but what you honestly think he would say when asked these questions.

1. What kind of work ethic does he have?

Are you the guy we have to beg to come in the weight room over the summer? Are you the player that coaches assign another guy to in order to make sure you are doing what you are supposed to be doing on your own? Or are you Mr. Reliable? Do you show up every day ready to work? Are you the first to finish in running drills? Do coaches have to encourage you every day to practice hard, run hard, lift hard, and play hard?

I have not met many college coaches who want to recruit a guy that does not have a good work ethic. They want guys they can coach to play football, they don't have a lot of patience for guys they have to coach to work hard. If you want to be a college football player that should be a given. It is to competitive, and very few guys have so much talent they can afford to be lazy. When guys like Randy Moss go on ESPN and say, "I play hard when I want to" it sets a terrible example for young players trying to advance and using football as a vehicle. When the college coach asks your high school coach, "What kind of work ethic does _____ have?" Make sure you have proven by your actions that your work ethic is second to none.

2. What are his strengths and weaknesses?

Everybody is good at some things and bad at others. The key is to maximize your strengths and negate your weaknesses. However, you must first identify what you need to improve.

For example, I knew I was slow before I went to the University Iowa Football camp. It's not like all of a sudden I realized after the coach told me my 40 time that I said, "huh, that's why I could never catch anyone at recess!" I knew that when I took a bad angle for a linebacker, I could not catch him. I knew that before I was a center, and I was late on the snap count, I was toast. So through experience, I learned that as a center I had to do three things to overcome my genetics, I needed to learn how to snap and step at the same time, narrow my stance, and use angles. By snapping and stepping at the same time I could gain a step on the defense. They would have to wait for the ball to move before they could react, I didn't. I could react as the ball was moving, and it made a huge difference. Second, I narrowed my stance. This enabled that first step I took to cover more ground. Now not only was getting a head start, but now I was making the most out of that head start. Third, I learned to go where people were going to be instead of where they were at right now. I knew the plays inside and out and I knew where the defense would run to try to stop the play, I tried to beat them to that point. This is what we call being a smart football player.

When faced with my speed challenge, a lot of people would say brilliant things like, "Why don't you just get faster?" What a fantastic idea! I had never thought of that. Get faster, brilliant. That would have saved me a lot of frustration. I blame my parents for my genetic limitations. I did everything I could to get faster. I jumped rope, did power cleans, lost weight, and even wore those ridiculous shoes for a while that look like reverse high heels. It all helped, but no amount of training was going to make me fast. I could become less slow, but never fast. Getting faster was only a limited option. When you are faced with your challenge, I encourage you to work on the obvious solution, but also be creative. What little things can you do to overcome your weaknesses, and turn them into positives?

What are the things you are not good at? You have to be honest with yourself. Sit down and make a list. Write it out on paper, this will help make it more real. Then make a plan. Ask for help from your high school coach if you need ideas. Research the internet, read books, find information any way to can to help overcome your shortcomings. Remember, nobody is good at everything and identifying your weaknesses is the first step to eliminating them.

3.   How tough is he?

Are you the guy who walks into the coach's office on Saturday morning after a tough Friday night game and says, "Coach, I have good news and bad news. The bad news is that last night I jammed my pinky between two shoulder pads and I am going to need to be excused from weight lifting today, practice on Monday, Tuesday, and Wednesday. However, the good news is that will be available for the Thursday walk-through and I will be able to play on Friday."

Football is a physical game and you are going to have aches and pains. If you are going to play this game for the next five years those aches and pains are only going to increase. The size of a football field has not changed since the game was invented, yet the players are bigger, stronger, faster and the collisions are much more violent. The human body can only take so much, but if you only practice on days you are 100%, you are not going to practice many days. In order to play this game you must be a tough guy. College coaches are looking for tough guys. They want guys that will battle, they want guys that will suck it up and play with some pain, they want guys that love the game and even kind of enjoy the pain a little, as crazy as that sounds. Are you a tough guy? More importantly, would your high school coach say you are? What have you done to demonstrate your toughness? What have you done that he would question your toughness? Nobody expects you to practice or play with a legitimate injury, but have you taken advantage of some situations to get out of having to practice or play? If you have, there is a pretty good chance your coach knows it too.

4.   How does he get along with his teammates?

I tell my players, "You either build people up or you tear people down. You are one or the other, you can't be both, who are you?" Are you the type of guy that every coach in America would like to have in his locker room? Do your teammates like you? Do they respect you? Do you know?

Every college coach is looking for players that will fit with the players he already has. He cannot go out and recruit a whole new team, so he looks at what he has now, and goes out and recruits guys that will help make him better on the field and in the locker room. He wants guys that make the team he has better. He wants players that will make the players he already has, better. That is what a good teammate does, he makes the other guys on the team around him better. The best example of this is Michael Jordan. He would not only score points and play defense, but he would make every guy on the floor better because of how good he was at scoring points and playing defense. Most people forget how good of a defensive player Jordan was in his prime. Most people remember the dunks, and acrobatics. I remember a picture up in the Kansas basketball locker room of Jordan in a defensive stance with the following message written underneath it, "My offense starts when the other team has the ball." Do you think the Bulls would have won six NBA championships if Michael Jordan didn't believe defense was important? I don't.

What kind of teammate are you? Do you make the others around you better by what you believe is important? If you are a skill guy, and another skill guy scores a touchdown, do you run to the end zone to congratulate him, or are you mad you didn't get the ball yourself? If you are defensive player, and another defensive player makes a big play, do you run over and congratulate him and celebrate his big play, or do you just go to the huddle or sideline?

Our team has a mission statement that outlines what is important to us as a football program. We identified teamwork and discipline as our two defining principles. We define teamwork as service. If you ask most people what it means to work as a team they will tell you they are able to work together, we call that cooperation. Real teamwork is serving one another. Here is an excerpt from the mission statement of the last team I coached:

Teamwork is based on service. A bad teammate asks what others can do for him, what coaches can do for him, what parents can do for him, he never looks to serve. A good teammate asks what he can do to help his peers, coaches, and parents. He understands that teamwork is about service, and not being served. We seek to serve each other. We understand that if we sacrifice ourselves to be a part of something bigger, we serve the team. We seek to be unselfish and think of the good of the group before our own personal glory, or selfish motives. We understand that by dedicating ourselves to one another we foster loyalty between teammates. This loyalty is not granted, but earned. Through service of one another, we build loyalty a little at a time. A good team serves one another.

A good teammate:

1. *Comes to all practices and football activities, because he understands that he cannot serve his teammates if he is not there.*
2. *Supports the players on the field during the game, because he understands the team's performance represents all our players, our coaches, our parents, and our school.*
3. *Does not abuse alcohol or drugs, because he understands these vices are counterproductive to the development of the team, and selfish in nature.*
4. *Conducts himself with class and dignity, because he understands that his actions influence the perception of the entire program.*

How good of a teammate are you? How well do you understand what it means to be a good teammate? What would your high school coach say?

5. What kind of leader is he?

One of the best ways to learn how to be a good follower is to have tried to be a leader. I know that I would be a much better assistant coach now, after being a head coach, than I was before. As a head coach I see how I want my assistants to work in our football program in a way I did not understand before I was in charge. Being a leader on your high school football team is kind of the same thing. As the best, or one of the best, players on your team you will be in a position of leadership, whether you are qualified or not. The other players will see you as a leader because you are a good player, and they will go where you take them. If you bust your butt in practice every day, you can bet a lot of them will too because they see you doing it. If you work hard in the weight room, other guys will too because they see you doing it. If you show you care about your team and your teammates, your teammates will too because they see you doing it. A lot of leadership is nonverbal. Sometimes what you do, speaks so loud it doesn't matter what you say.

Colleges are looking for leaders. Players who were leaders on their high school team will find it easier to follow when they are freshmen on their college team. They will know from the previous year the frustrations they had with various players to get them to do the right thing, and they will be self-motivated when they get to college. Colleges want players that have led their team to win games and championships. I have coached teams that were 0-10 and I have coached teams that were 9-1, and I can say with absolute certainty, more college coaches came around to recruit the players that helped us become 9-1 rather than the guys that made us 0-10. If you lead your team in practice, and you help them win games, you will have a greater chance of being recruited. I remember my college coach, Glen Mason, saying about our quarterback, Chip Hillary, that when Chip was in high school he was the captain of his football team, basketball team, and baseball team, and all those teams qualified for their state tournaments. That's what made him want to recruit him, he said, "I didn't know if he was a great quarterback, but I did know he was a great leader because he took three different sports teams to the state tournament." What kind of leader are you? What would your high school coach say?

Chapter 8
The Clearinghouse

One of the saddest things for a high school player is when they are offered a scholarship and they cannot accept it because they don't have the grades. Sometimes it's a case of missing classes, or an ACT or SAT test score that is too low, whatever the deficiency it's always sad when the have to turn it down. This chapter outlines the academic requirements to satisfy initial eligibility for the NCAA.

Core Classes
Every accredited high school is registered with the NCAA. If you go the website www.ncaaclearinghouse.net and find your high school you can see the list of approved core courses. It is referred to as Form 48H.

For the class of 2008 and beyond the athletes are required to have 16 core courses to be eligible as a freshman at a Division I institution. A Core GPA will be calculated based on the grades in these 16 courses and that GPA will be used to determine what ACT/SAT score will be needed.

The 16 courses needed are:
  4 years of English
  3 years of math (Algebra I or higher)
  2 years of natural/physical science (one must be a lab science)
  1 year additional English, math, or science
  2 years of social studies
    4 years of additional core courses (from any area listed above, or from foreign language, non-doctrinal religion or philosophy)

Usually, when a high school student gets a report card from his school it will have his grade point average (GPA) on it. This is your "Overall" GPA. The NCAA is not interested in this one, only your Core GPA based on the above classes. Here is a worksheet that will help you calculate it, and a sample to see how it is done. I encourage you to always have your high school guidance counselor do it too. They have more experience and it will double check your calculations and help you plan for ways it can improve.

16 Core Courses GPA Calculation

A = 4.0 B = 3.0   C = 2.0   D = 1.0   F = 0

16 Core Courses

English – 4 Years
English #1: _____ 1st Sem. Grade: _____ 2nd Sem. Grade: _____ Points: _____
English #2: _____ 1st Sem. Grade: _____ 2nd Sem. Grade: _____ Points: _____
English #3: _____ 1st Sem. Grade: _____ 2nd Sem. Grade: _____ Points: _____
English #4: _____ 1st Sem. Grade: _____ 2nd Sem. Grade: _____ Points: _____

Math – 3 Years of Algebra I or Higher
Math #1: _____ 1st Sem. Grade: _____ 2nd Sem. Grade: _____ Points: _____
Math #2: _____ 1st Sem. Grade: _____ 2nd Sem. Grade: _____ Points: _____
Math #3: _____ 1st Sem. Grade: _____ 2nd Sem. Grade: _____ Points: _____

Science – 2 Years of Science (1 must be a Lab Science)
Science #1: _____ 1st Sem. Grade: _____ 2nd Sem. Grade: _____ Points: _____
Science #2: _____ 1st Sem. Grade: _____ 2nd Sem. Grade: _____ Points: _____

Additional Credit (Need only *ONE* of the following)
English #5: _____ 1st Sem. Grade: _____ 2nd Sem. Grade: _____ Points: _____
Math #3: _____ 1st Sem. Grade: _____ 2nd Sem. Grade: _____ Points: _____
Science #3: _____ 1st Sem. Grade: _____ 2nd Sem. Grade: _____ Points: _____

Social Science – 2 Years
Social Science #1: _____ 1st Sem. Grade: _____ 2nd Sem. Grade: _____ Points:
_____
Social Science #2: _____ 1st Sem. Grade: _____ 2nd Sem. Grade: _____ Points:
_____

Additional Courses – 4 Years
These courses can come from English, Math, Science, Social Studies, Foreign Language,
non-doctrinal religion, philosophy, or computer science.
Credit #1: _____ 1st Sem. Grade: _____ 2nd Sem. Grade: _____ Points: _____
Credit #2: _____ 1st Sem. Grade: _____ 2nd Sem. Grade: _____ Points: _____
Credit #3: _____ 1st Sem. Grade: _____ 2nd Sem. Grade: _____ Points: _____
Credit #4: _____ 1st Sem. Grade: _____ 2nd Sem. Grade: _____ Points: _____

Total Number of Points Earned: _____

Core GPA = Total Points Earned / Number of Grades (32)

(SAMPLE) 16 Core Courses GPA Calculation

A = 4.0 B = 3.0   C = 2.0   D = 1.0   F = 0

16 Core Courses

English – 4 Years
English #1: English 9   1st Sem. Grade: __B__   2nd Sem. Grade: __C__   Points: __5__

English #2: English 10 1st Sem. Grade: __C__   2nd Sem. Grade: __D__   Points: __3__

English #3: English 11 1st Sem. Grade: __A__   2nd Sem. Grade: __B__   Points: __7__

English #4: Drama I   1st Sem. Grade: __A__   2nd Sem. Grade: __A__   Points: __8__

Math – 2 Years of Algebra I or Higher
Math #1: Algebra I   1st Sem. Grade: __C__   2nd Sem. Grade: __C__   Points: __4__

Math #2: Geometry   1st Sem. Grade: __C__   2nd Sem. Grade: __B__   Points: __5__

Math #2: Algebra II   1st Sem. Grade: __C__   2nd Sem. Grade: __B__   Points: __5__

Science – 2 Years of Science (1 must be a Lab Science)
Science #1: Earth Science   1st Sem. Grade: __D__   2nd Sem. Grade: __C__   Points: __3__

Science #2: Biology   1st Sem. Grade: __C__   2nd Sem. Grade: __C__   Points: __4__

Additional Credit (Need only *ONE* of the following)
English #5: _____   1st Sem. Grade: _____   2nd Sem. Grade: _____   Points: _____
Math #3: _____   1st Sem. Grade: _____   2nd Sem. Grade: _____   Points: _____
Science #3: Chemistry   1st Sem. Grade: __A__   2nd Sem. Grade: __A__   Points: __8__

Social Science – 2 Years
Social Science #1: US History   1st Sem. Grade: __A__   2nd Sem. Grade: __A__   Points: __8__
Social Science #2: Gov/Econ   1st Sem. Grade: __B__   2nd Sem. Grade: __A__   Points: __7__

Additional Courses – 3 Years
These courses can come from English, Math, Science, Social Studies, Foreign Language, non-doctrinal religion, philosophy, or computer science.
Credit #1: English 12   1st Sem. Grade: __B__   2nd Sem. Grade: __B__   Points: __6__
Credit #2: Pre-Calculus   1st Sem. Grade: __A__   2nd Sem. Grade: __A__   Points: __8__
Credit #3: World History   1st Sem. Grade: __A__   2nd Sem. Grade: __A__   Points: __8__
Credit #3: Physics   1st Sem. Grade: __A__   2nd Sem. Grade: __A__   Points: __8__

Total Number of Points Earned: ___97___

Core GPA = Total Points Earned / Number of Grades (32)
Core GPA = 97/32 = 3.03

Tips to Improve Your Core GPA:

1. Educate yourself on what the NCAA will accept as a core class from your school. For example, at Roosevelt High School in Des Moines, Iowa you can get an English credit for Drama or Forensics. When I learned this and asked my players if they knew that their Drama class could be counted as an English credit, all of them were surprised. When I was in high school I wrote for the newspaper and yearbook, and that counted as an English credit. Go to the NCAA Clearinghouse website and look up your high school and see what classes are eligible for core credits. Focus on those classes when planning your schedule. The NCAA sets a minimum number needed, there is no penalty for taking too many. Which leads to tip #2.

2. Your Core GPA will be calculated based on your best 16 credits, depending on the year you enter college, so retake a class you received a poor grade in or take another course to replace a low grade. For example, I coached a young man that when he came to high school did not do very well academically his freshman year. In his freshman science course, Physical Science, he got a "C" first semester and a "D" second semester. It was not an issue of him being smart enough, he just did not apply himself at the start of high school and got a poor grade as a result. He took Biology as a sophomore and did well. He earned a "B" each semester. His junior year he took Chemistry and got an "A" first semester and a "B" second semester. Prior to his senior year he asked me what I thought he should take as a senior. He showed an aptitude for science and wanted to take a class to replace the poor grade he received as a freshman, so I encouraged him to take Physics. I taught the class at the time and I knew he could do well because he had done well in Chemistry and Biology. He ended up getting an "A" each semester and we used that as his lab class. Chemistry was his other science credit, and he used the Biology credits as one of his additional core courses needed. He was offered a scholarship by a Big 12 school and even though his ACT score was low, he qualified because his GPA was so high.

3. Summer school. If your district offers summer school, you should go. Summer school credits count just as much and the ones during the regular school year and they are usually easier to earn. It is also easier for some students to do well in summer school because they are only taking one or two courses and they can just focus on those classes rather than trying to juggle six or seven classes at once. In addition, most schools around the country don't offer summer sports so the athlete can just focus for three or four

weeks on school and pound out a summer class and earn a good grade in the process. Summer school is only good before graduation. Once you graduate in the spring of your senior year, any credits you earn the following summer cannot be used towards initial freshman eligibility.

Once you have determined what your core GPA, now you need to see what standardize test score you need to become eligible by NCAA standards. It works on a sliding scale so the higher your core GPA, the lower your minimum test score. Many kids I have worked with do not test well; as a result I encourage them to get the highest possible GPA so the test score is more a formality than a necessity.

Starting in 2015-16 school year the NCAA instituted a partial qualifier status based on their academic performance. To be eligible to participate in competition as a freshman, a prospective student athlete will need to have a GPA of 2.3 and an SAT score of 1080 or ACT summative score of 93. The summative score on the ACT is calculated by adding the sub score on each of the four sections; reading, English, math, and science. Review the enclosed chart to see what score you need, based on your core GPA.

Sliding Scale

GPA for Aid and Practice	GPA for Competition	SAT Score	ACT Sum
3.550	4.000	400	37
3.450	3.900	440	41
3.350	3.800	480	43
3.250	3.700	520	46
3.150	3.600	560	48
3.030	3.500	600	50
2.950	3.400	640	53
2.850	3.300	680	56
2.750	3.200	720	59
2.650	3.100	760	62
2.550	3.000	800	66
2.450	2.900	840	70
2.350	2.800	880	73
2.250	2.700	920	77
2.150	2.600	960	81
2.050	2.500	1000	85
2.000	2.450	1020	86
NA	2.400	1040	88
NA	2.300	1080	93

Tips To Get The Best Standardized Test Score:

1. Take the test early and often. Some of you may be looking at the ACT scores on the sliding scale and panicking because you thought the best possible score was a 36 and you see that you need an 85. The NCAA can be tough, but not that tough. On the ACT there are four test categories; English, Reading, Math, and Science Reasoning. In each category you will get a score from 1 – 36. If you add your score for each test together, that's how you get the number on the sliding scale. For example, if your core GPA is 2.500 and you need an 85, then all you have to do is average a 22 on each test. The SAT works the same way by combining your score from the Critical Reading (formerly known as the verbal) and Math sections. If you struggle with standardized tests then start taking the test your sophomore year. The NCAA does not penalize you for taking it multiple times and it will take your best score on each test. That means even if your overall score went down, but you scored better on one section you can take that score and replace a lower one on a previous test.

   Here is an example:
   First Time - ACT Test
   Reading – 22
   English – 22
   Math – 18
   Science Reasoning – 20
   Composite – 80

   Second Time – ACT Test
   Reading – 22
   English – 23
   Math – 14
   Science Reasoning – 22
   Composite – 79

   ACT Best Scores
   Reading – 22
   English – 23
   Math – 18
   Science Reasoning – 22
   Composite – 85

Even though when you took the test the second time your score went down in Math, stayed the same in Reading, but improved it in English and Math, your composite score will go up. The NCAA allows you to create your best composite score by combining your best sub-scores on each section of the ACT.

Research shows, the more you take a test, the better you will do on it. The ACT is offered about 5 times a year and the SAT is about 7 times. Find out when the next one is offered and sign up to take them. Start taking it your sophomore year. Don't waste your money on the PSAT unless you are a candidate for National Honor Society or a National Merit Scholar or another organization that requires a PSAT score. Go ahead and start taking the ACT and SAT. There is no penalty, and your scores will probably go up with each attempt.

2. Prepare to take the test. Invest in a book or online program that has similar questions to the ACT or SAT. Learn the test taking strategies associated with taking a standardized test. It's a lot like Las Vegas; you find ways to increase your chances of winning. Taking a standardized test is not always about choosing the right answer, sometimes it's about eliminating the wrong ones. If you read a question and you are not sure about the answer then start eliminating the ones you think are wrong. On each question there are usually four options, that means that if you guessed you would have a 25% chance of getting the question right. If you eliminate one possibility your odds go up to one out of three, 33%. If you can eliminate two answers then its 50-50 you get it right. Each time you eliminate one, your odds of getting it right go up. Invest in an ACT or SAT prep book and it will have other ways you can increase your score.

3. Take both tests. Most people only take one test. Since the tests are structured different they will appeal to different types of test takers. You will score better on one than the other and if you are on the bubble academically it could be a big enough difference to make you eligible for a scholarship. It costs around $40 to take each one each time and it is money well spent. Think of it as a small investment with a potential huge payoff, a football scholarship.

In order to be eligible to practice, play, and get a scholarship at a Division I school you must do four things.
1. Graduate from high school.
2. Complete your core courses with a passing grade in each.
3. Present a minimum GPA in those core courses.

4.   Present a qualifying test score on either the ACT or SAT test.

At the completion of your Junior year you should register with the NCAA Clearinghouse. In order to do that you need to go to the website www.ncaaclearinghouse.net and get a form to register or do it online. Then have your high school send an official six-semester transcript and have ACT or SAT testing company send them your scores. Review their "List of Approved Core Courses" and make sure that all of your core classes are present. If any are missing, see your counselor and make sure it is updated with the NCAA. Once you are registered you will need to complete a Student Release form so they can review your grades. There is a small fee to apply to the Clearinghouse. Now all you have to do is complete your core courses, obtain an acceptable standardized test score and graduate from high school.

Chapter 9
Official Visits

A visit to a college campus should be viewed as a job interview. You are trying to get the job, while at the same time you are trying to decide if you should take the job if it's offered. Too many times student athletes fumble the ball here and they look at these trips as either an early "Spring Break" vacation or a "Who Can Cater To My Ego The Most" weekend. Both views are misguided.

As a high school senior I took a recruiting trip to Iowa State. At the time they were not a very good program and I thought they would be lucky to have me. I arrogantly went on my trip and did my best to be unimpressed with their campus, their football facilities, their current players, and their coaches. As a result, when I met with their head coach at the time, Jim Walden, he was equally unimpressed with me and did not offer me a scholarship. When I went back to school on Monday my high school head coach called me into his office and asked how my visit went the previous weekend. I lied and told him it went well. Then he said, "That's interesting, because I just got off the phone with the Iowa State coaches and they said it was terrible and they are not going to recruit you now. They said you seemed bored all weekend and they did not think you would fit in with their current players." I was floored. How could a program that needed me as bad as they did, now no longer want me? Like most things in recruiting when I went through it, I didn't get it.

The visit is not all about getting you to go there. Part of the visit is to see if you will fit in with the players they already have on the team. If you go on campus and none of the current players like you, then they can't recruit you. If you go there with a negative attitude, they won't recruit you. If you go there determined to be unimpressed then you will do nothing to impress them either. I went on my trip with the attitude they had to win me over, I went with the "Who Can Cater to My Ego The Most" attitude.

Here are some tips that should help you with this process, and increase your chances of leaving your visit with a scholarship offer every time.

NCAA Rule:

You are allowed five official visits. An official visit means the school can pay for your transportation there, your hotel, your food, and your entertainment while on campus. The school cannot pay the transportation cost of your parents, but once they are on campus they can provide a hotel room and pay for their food and entertainment. If you live far enough away to fly, then your parents will have to pay for their own plane ticket. However, if you live close enough to drive, then the school will give you a stipend based on your mileage and your parents can ride in the car with you and in essence the school pays for their transportation too. The school, or any booster of the school, cannot give you anything you can take with you back home. This includes hats, t-shirts, sweatshirts, shoes, or anything else that could be considered a gift. You are welcome to stop at the bookstore during your trip and purchase some of these things, but they cannot be received as gifts.

Prior to your visit you are required to provide an up-to-date transcript and any ACT or SAT testing scores you have earned. In addition, most D-IAA and D-II school will have you fill out some financial aid information to determine what grants you may qualify for in order to put together a financial estimate on what it will cost to go there. Remember that D-I schools can only offer full scholarships, but D-IAA and D-II can combine football scholarship money with Pell Grants and other scholarships available.

Typical Recruiting Visit:
Saturday
- **Arrive on Campus and Tour**
  - If you fly in, then a coach will pick you up at the airport and take you to campus. Sometimes you may fly in on Friday night because there is not an

early flight on Saturday. Once you get on campus they will have someone give you a tour. You will have an opportunity to see the buildings you could be taking classes in, the football stadium, weight room, indoor facility, dining hall, academic center, and dormitories. If there is anything you want to see that they don't show you, make sure you ask and they will take you to it if they have one.

- Lunch
  - Most times you will eat lunch with your position coach. He may be the one that picked you up from the airport so this may be your second contact. This is a good opportunity for you and your parents to ask questions about the football program and the coach that you will be working with most closely. Sometimes the coach that recruits you is not your position coach. Most coaching staffs divide up the country or state and you could be recruited by the defensive line coach and you are a quarterback. You will have talked to him multiple times on the telephone so you will have a relationship with him already. In addition, he will be the one that came to your high school and arranged for this visit so he may be at lunch as well. He may be at lunch too, along with your position coach if he does not have a player at his position visiting. Some schools will do a buffet lunch in an on-campus building and some will go to a restaurant, it all depends on what facilities they have available. Relax and be yourself and enjoy the meal and be social.
- **Meet with Academic Advisor**
  - Prior to your visit the coach recruiting you will ask you what you may be interested in studying if you come to that college. Based on what you tell them the school will hook you up with an academic advisor. This is usually a faculty member in the area of study you are interested in pursuing. They will go through what you will need to do to obtain a degree in that field. Feel free to ask them to lay out a four year plan that most athletes would follow to pursue that degree.

Get their contact information so you can ask questions later if you have them, or use them as a resource once you are on campus. This is a great contact to have and keep throughout your time at the school.

- **Meet with Position Coach**
  - This meeting is usually done in the office of the coach. He will go through what offense or defense they operate. Some coaches will show film. This is a football meeting. He will ask you some questions to gauge your knowledge and determine how easily you could learn their system. In addition, he will usually talk about the current players they have on their team and where you will fit in if you come on campus. It is appropriate to ask about when you would possibly play and if they think you would be red-shirted. Again, relax and be yourself and look at this as a job interview with your potential supervisor.

- **Dinner**
  - This dinner will again either be an on-campus building or at a restaurant depending on their facilities and what the recruiting philosophy. At this point you will probably meet your player-host. This is a person who is a current player and he will be your guide for the night. The coach recruiting you will usually pick a guy on the team that he thinks you would get along with best. There could be a connection because you are from the same hometown or high school. It could be that you will play the same position in college. It could be the college coach thinks you have similar personalities and this college player is someone you will feel comfortable around. Whatever the reason, you will usually meet this person during dinner. Your parents will have an opportunity to ask him questions and it is usually a nice meal.

- **Spend Time with Player Host**
  - After dinner the coaches will usually take the parents to either another social event or back to the hotel depending on their preference and the

player-host will take out the recruit. Depending on what you like to do the player-host will usually take you back to where he lives and you will have a chance to meet some other players. Then a lot of things can happen from here. I have heard about or experienced the following activities with player-hosts and recruits:

- Going to a movie
- Going to a house party around campus
- Using a fake ID and going to a bar
- Hanging out at the host's house and talking to players
- Going to a strip club
- Going to a campus event like a basketball game or show
- Playing poker
- Going to a casino
- Getting drunk or doing drugs

I give my players two pieces of advice before they leave:

1. Know who you are before you leave and don't forget who you are while you are there.

2. Don't do anything on Friday night that you would not want to read about on Saturday morning in the newspaper.

If you don't want to do something don't let some player-host talk you into something you don't want to do. On every team in college football there are; partiers, scholars, Christians, drinkers, drug users, good guys, and troublemakers. Football attracts all kinds of people and you can fit in with any team because you will find the guys most like you, and that will be your group through college. This is the part of the visit most guys look forward to the most, and it's the one I worry about. Be safe and don't do anything that could jeopardize you having an opportunity to get your education paid for playing for that school.

Sunday

- Breakfast

- The college coaches usually schedule this early in the morning in hopes that you will not be out to late the night before. This breakfast is usually at an on-campus building, restaurant, or hotel depending on the facilities available. At this meal it is usually your parents and the position or recruiting coach. This is a good opportunity to ask any questions you may have forgotten to ask the day before and you thought of later.
  - Meet with Head Coach
    - This meeting could take place at breakfast or it could be in the office of the head coach. This is where you will talk money. If you are going to get offered a scholarship it will be at this point. The assistant coaches can talk about offering scholarships but there is only one person I trust when it comes to that; it's the head coach. If it is a D-IAA or D-II school they take your financial information and put together a package to estimate what it will cost you to go to school. They may ask you about other offers you have on the table and I would encourage you to make yourself as attractive as possible. If it is a D-I school it will be an all or nothing offer. When I went to Iowa State I had a poor visit and left without an offer, when I went to Kansas I had a great visit and left with an offer. Most school are on a tight recruiting budget and will only offer a visit to guys they are going to offer, so usually if you get an invitation to visit then a scholarship offer is coming, if it has not already.
  - Go Home
    - Depending on how you got to campus will determine how you get home. If you flew in then a coach will take you to the airport. If you drove you will now drive home too. Either way, be sure to thank the coach recruiting you and the head coach for inviting you on the visit. If you did not commit make sure you ask a timetable that you need to make a decision and always leave on good terms.

This is a typical recruiting visit. Sometimes they will have a basketball game on campus on Saturday afternoon and that will change the order of things, but most visits include all of these items in some order.

Tips for a Great Official Visit:

1. Bring your parents. Some players hate to hear this suggestion. They view the recruiting trip an early "Spring Break Girls Gone Wild" vacation and they don't want mom and dad spoiling their good time. There will be enough time for that type of stuff later. Your parents can be your best advocate and most times they have the most invested in you as a person, so it only makes sense to include them on what will be one of the biggest decisions you will make in your lifetime. They will be a little more objective and will not get caught up in the moment like a lot of guys do on the trip. It may create a financial hardship to get the money for airfare, but if at all possible try to make it work. In addition, if you mother is anything like mine, you will have to tell her everything about the trip anyway, so you might as well bring her.

2. Come with empty pockets and leave with empty pockets.
   Come with empty pockets.

   I would encourage you to leave your cell phone, headphones, and hand held games at home or in the hotel. A college coach told me a story of a recruit they had on campus that kept playing his phone all the way though the tour of campus, basketball game, and dinner. He became so frustrated with the recruit that he encouraged the head coach to not offer him a scholarship because he did not seem interested in the school.
   Leave with empty pockets.

   Don't accept a $50 sweatshirt that could cost you a $100,000 scholarship. It is not worth it. Recruiting violations could cost you an opportunity to go there and it could get the school in trouble too. If you are offered something, politely turn it down. Keep your eye on the big picture.

3. Spend as much time with players as possible. When you have time to spend with the player-host ask him to introduce you to the other players that will play your position. Ask them about your position coach and head coach. Ask them about the atmosphere on the team. Ask them the questions you may be hesitant to ask the coaches. They went through the same

process you are going through so ask them about that as well. See if you think you could fit in with these guys. The coaching staff could get fired the day after the next season; the players will not. Get to know them and see if you could see yourself with them next year.

4. Relax, be humble, and have fun. Nobody likes the guy who comes on campus and thinks he is the next big thing. I can remember as a player-host and seeing those recruits come on trips and the other players and I would start counting the days until practice started and we could put him in his place. Great players that are beloved are usually humble. If you are the next big thing then let other people say it, you shouldn't have to. Remember that you are on a business trip to determine whether or not you are going to get paid to play a game in exchange for an education so show some personality and be someone they would like to have on their team.

5. Don't embarrass yourself, your family, or your school by making a poor decision. It may seem like a good idea at the time to drink a bottle of whiskey, smoke some marijuana, and break into some house to steal some DVD movies or something like that, it will not seem like such a good idea at breakfast on Sunday. If you are on this trip then you are one of the 20 – 25 potential student-athletes they are going to sign up of a five-year all expense paid scholarship, a chance to change your life forever, don't blow it on something stupid.

Chapter 10
Scholarship Offers &
Commitments

Scholarship Offers

A full-ride football scholarship will change your life. There is no doubt in my mind; I have seen it first-hand. Without a football scholarship, I may have gone into my dad's construction business. If I had gone to college it would not have been two states away and I would never have met my wife and I would not have my kids. I would have taken out student loans and years later would still be paying them back to the government. Instead I went to school and graduated debt free, I got to play major college football, go to the Aloha Bowl in Hawaii and play against the eventual national champions in the Kick-Off Classic in Giants Stadium on national television. A full-ride football scholarship certainly changed my life. Every time one of my players get their first offer I always say, "This offer will change your life."

Colleges can offer a scholarship at any time. I have seen scholarships offered many ways: in person; over the telephone; on email; by fax; through a certified letter; by FedEx; in a text message; and by using the high school coach as a messenger. There is no "right" way to get offered a scholarship. There is also no "right" time to get offered a scholarship. I have seen scholarship offers come: before their junior season; before their senior season; at a spring unofficial visit; at summer camp; during the one phone call in May; during their junior season; during their senior season; on their recruiting trip; after their recruiting trip; on

National Signing Day; after National Signing Day. A scholarship offer is kind of like lightning, it can strike anywhere at any time.

Here are some tips to help you with scholarship offers:

1. Ask the question. If you are concerned that a school may be stringing you along and they are not going to offer a scholarship, then ask the question, "Are you going to offer me a football scholarship?" Student-athletes are often afraid to ask this question because they fear it will decrease their chances of getting an offer, totally untrue. If you are good enough, and they need you, then you will get an offer. If a school has not offered right away then it usually means you are not their number one choice. They may be going after someone else and you are second or third on their list. The good news is that a lot of schools are also going after that guy whose number one, and only one school will get him, so if you are not number one right away you can move up in hurry when other players start committing. Sometimes just asking the question opens a dialog and you can see where you stand with a school and it will relieve some of your stress.

2. Don't expect every school to offer. I tell my players to be surprised every time a school offers a scholarship. If you expect everyone to offer, then you will spend most of the recruiting process disappointed. There will be about 100 guys nationwide who will get most of the attention in recruiting. Those 100 guys will get offers from everywhere. If you are one of those 100 guys, then ignore this suggestion. However, remember there are 119 D-I schools and they each sign about 25 players a year, which totals about 2975 players. The top 100 or so get most of the attention, the other 2875 will get a handful of offers each. Remember, not every D-I recruit gets an offer to play at every D-I school, be happy with every offer you get.

3. Not every school is funded the same, know the difference between divisions. In Chapter 1 there is a list of every division and every conference, make sure you know where the school you are talking to falls, it will determine how much money they have to offer. Remember:

   • 128 D-I schools with 85 scholarships each, assuming they are not on probation. Those scholarships are all, or nothing. You either get; tuition, books, room & board, fees, or you get nothing. There is no such thing as a partial scholarship to a D-I school. In addition, starting in 2014 schools are allowed to provide a monthly stipend to players called a "Cost of Attendance" stipend. The stipend supposed to be based on the tuition of the school, proximity to an airport, and other transportation costs. One additional question recruits will start to ask during recruiting will be what their monthly stipend will be at each school. As you will see in the chart below, not all schools are equal. Listed below is the 2014 "Cost of Attendance" stipend for the Power 5 conferences.

School	14-15 Stipend	Monthly Stipend	Conference
Tennessee	$5,666	$630	SEC
Auburn	$5,586	$621	SEC
UCLA	$5,562	$618	PAC 12
Louisville	$5,202	$578	ACC
Utah	$5,166	$574	PAC 12
Mississippi State	$5,126	$570	SEC
Texas Tech	$5,100	$567	Big 12
Penn State	$4,788	$532	Big 10
Cal	$4,718	$524	PAC 12
TCU	$4,700	$522	Big 12
Oklahoma	$4,614	$513	Big 12
Oklahoma State	$4,560	$507	Big 12
Ole Miss	$4,500	$500	SEC
Texas	$4,310	$479	Big 12
Wisconsin	$4,265	$474	Big 10
South Carolina	$4,151	$461	SEC
K-State	$4,112	$457	Big 12
Arizona	$4,074	$453	PAC 12
Arkansas	$4,002	$445	SEC
Florida State	$3,884	$432	ACC
Baylor	$3,882	$431	Big 12
Missouri	$3,664	$407	SEC
Colorado	$3,626	$403	PAC 12
Clemson	$3,608	$401	ACC
Nebraska	$3,544	$394	Big 10
Washington State	$3,542	$394	PAC 12

Florida	$3,320	$369	SEC
Pittsburg	$3,300	$367	ACC
Stanford	$3,215	$357	PAC 12
Arizona State	$3,154	$350	PAC 12
LSU	$3,096	$344	SEC
Kansas	$3,076	$342	Big 12
Indiana	$3,026	$336	Big 10
Maryland	$3,024	$336	Big 10
Alabama	$2,892	$321	SEC
Oregon State	$2,856	$317	PAC 12
Miami	$2,780	$309	ACC
Vanderbilt	$2,780	$309	SEC
Virgina Tech	$2,770	$308	ACC
Rutgers	$2,763	$307	Big 10
Texas A&M	$2,706	$301	SEC
Washington	$2,679	$298	PAC 12
Georgia	$2,598	$289	SEC
Virginia	$2,565	$285	ACC
Illinois	$2,500	$278	Big 10
Ohio State	$2,454	$273	Big 10
NC State	$2,430	$270	ACC
Iowa State	$2,420	$269	Big 12
Wake Forrest	$2,400	$267	ACC
Oregon	$2,340	$260	PAC 12
Northwestern	$2,326	$258	Big 10
North Carolina	$2,236	$248	ACC
Duke	$2,206	$245	ACC
Minnesota	$2,194	$244	Big 10
Iowa	$2,128	$236	Big 10
Michigan	$2,054	$228	Big 10
West Virginia	$1,971	$219	Big 12
Notre Dame	$1,950	$217	IND
Purdue	$1,920	$213	Big 10
Michigan State	$1,870	$208	Big 10

Georgia Tech	$1,720	$191	ACC
Syracuse	$1,632	$181	ACC
USC	$1,580	$176	PAC 12
Boston College	$1,400	$156	ACC

- 125 D-IAA schools with 63 equivalents each. Notice the word equivalent, and not the word scholarship. Some schools are funded as an in-state equivalent rate, and will have less money to offer than a school funded at an out-of-state equivalent rate. The equivalents can be divided up. With only 63 equivalents to spread around to 90 or so players, not everyone is on a full athletic scholarship. That doesn't mean they have to pay to go to school. Most times these schools will have each player will out financial assistance forms and whatever their grants and non-athletic scholarships don't cover, they use football money to pay. This helps their funding go further. As a result, most schools at this level will ask you to fill out those financial forms before they offer so they can put together the best package possible for you to consider.

- 170 D-II schools with 36 equivalents each. The same issues apply to D-II as apply to D-IAA, but now there is even less football money to go around. Most players at this level have to pay part of their way to go to school.

4. Have a response ready in case you get offered a scholarship. Sometimes guys panic when they get offered a scholarship. They don't know what to say so they make a commitment they are not ready to make because they are afraid to disappoint the college coach. When offered a scholarship you should say one of the two following things:

- "Thank you, I will take it." If the school that just offered you is your number one choice, a school you have been dreaming about playing at since you were a little kid, then take it and run. Everyone has a number one choice in their mind, the school who's offer you would drop everything and go to, if that school just offered, take it. Turn in your ticket and the game is over for you. Count your blessings, most guys will not fall in your category.

- "Thank you. How long do I have to make a decision?" It the school that just offered does not fall in category number one, use this response. This response gives you something to say, and it also provides some information that will help you make a decision. The offer may be good until signing day, it may be good until Monday, you don't know unless you ask. I have had guys playing for me get offered and then call a couple of months later call to accept it, and the offer was no longer any good. When I asked them if they asked the coach how long the offer stood, neither had asked so we didn't have many options. Always remember, if this school is the only school that offers, then I guarantee they will be your number one choice on signing day.

5.   Alibi your parents. If a college coach has offered you a scholarship and is pressing for a commitment, the one thing they can never argue with is the following statement, "I would really like to talk to my parents some more about it." You should include your parents in this process anyway, but this gives you a way out of what can sometimes be a difficult situation.

Commitments

There are two types of commitments in recruiting: non-binding verbal commitment and your National Letter of Intent. A verbal commitment can be given at any time, but your National Letter of Intent can only be signed after the first Wednesday in February of your senior year.

Scenario #1 – Verbal Commitment

A high school junior is offered a scholarship by a Big 12 school and decides the summer before his senior football season that he is going to accept the scholarship. The Big 12 head football coach assures him that if he is injured during his senior season that he will still honor the scholarship offer and will reward him for his early commitment with some peace of mind that his future with the school is secure. The athlete has made a verbal commitment; he has not signed any document tying him to the school.

Commonly Asked Questions:

1. Can the school rescind the offer?

      • Yes. Their offer is also non-binding. Most of the time they will not rescind it for a poor season or an injury, but if the athlete is arrested or does something to embarrass the high school or future college, then you will see the college take back the offer.

2. Can the athlete change his mind and go somewhere else?

      • Yes. The commitment is also non-binding, and if you decide you want to go somewhere else, then there is nothing forcing you to sign with that school. Sometimes if an athlete makes a commitment and there is a coaching change after the season, the athlete will decide to re-enter the recruiting process.

3.   If I am committed to one school can I still take visits to other schools?

- Yes you can, but why would you want to. If you have made a commitment you should keep it. If you still want to visit other schools, then don't make a commitment. Be a man of your word and if you commit to someone, keep it. I once heard a Big 12 coach describe it to a recruit like this after the recruit made a verbal commitment prior to his senior season. "Recruiting is kind of like dating. I love you, and you love me, and we are going to get married. This is our engagement. You don't want to do anything during our engagement that would make me not want to get married to you and you don't want me to do anything that would make you not want to marry me. On the first Wednesday in February we are going to get married, please don't cheat on me." Good advice.

4.   If I make a verbal commitment will other schools stop recruiting me?

- Unfortunately not. To some schools it is a sign that you are worth recruiting. Their job is to get the best players possible and some figure if you are good enough for the school you are committed to then you would be good enough for them too. They start calling, writing, text messaging, and sending more and more mail. There is nothing you can do, other than to keep telling them you are happy with your choice and you are not interested in looking around.

5.   If I get hurt, will they really still give me a scholarship?

- In most cases, yes. It is terrible public relations on their part if they make the offer, with that specific assurance, and then rescind the offer due to injury. If the injury is career ending they can always sign you up and then have you medically disqualified. The same is true if you get injured in college. If you are injured and cannot play anymore they will medically disqualify you and you get to keep your scholarship. By doing it this way it does not count as one of the 85 they have to field a team.

Scenario #2 – Letter of Intent

A high school senior signs a National Letter of Intent to play at a Big 10 school.

Commonly Asked Questions:

1. Can I lose my scholarship?

   - Yes. It is not a guaranteed contract. If you are arrested, break an NCAA rule by accepting money from a booster, or do something else that may embarrass the university, then you will loose your scholarship.

2. How long is my scholarship last?

   - One year. Each year you will sign a financial aid agreement for the coming school year. Most people think you are signing a five year contract on National Signing Day, but you do not. Your scholarship is renewed annually and at the D-IAA and D-II levels the amount of money you receive from football usually changes each year. Most coaches will tell you it is good for five years, and that is what you will get provided if you maintain your good-standing with the University and the football program. Some athletes will graduate in four years and then during their fifth year start a graduate level program while they finish playing. At KU, the education program is five years with the student teaching, so when I finished playing I started taking night and summer classes for my graduate program. At the end of my fifth year I had earned a masters degree while completing my student teaching. In addition, our academic advisors helped me apply for a Hitachi Fellowship that enabled me to get a second masters degree. One scholarship turned into one undergraduate and two post-graduate degrees. Some athletes go into it thinking this will last forever; I encourage you to look at like a race against time. Picture the sand falling through an hourglass while you are pursuing your degree or degrees, your goal should be to get all the education you can before the sand runs out.

3. What happens if I get hurt and cannot play?

   - If a doctor determines that you cannot play, and medically disqualifies you, you will keep your scholarship. The team then does not have to count your scholarship as one of their 85, and they can offer another scholarship to another player. Also, if are injured in football the college will pay for any medical treatment required for that injury. In 1995 when I injured my back at KU I did not have health insurance.

They paid for my surgery, my hospital stay, my medications, everything. I later learned the University takes out a supplemental health insurance policy on its athletes to cover any expenses not covered by their own insurance.

4. Can I change schools later?

    *   Yes. If you transfer to another D-I school you will lose one year of eligibility. If you transfer to a D-IAA or D-II you are eligible right away.

5. If I sign a Letter of Intent, does that mean I am in the school?

    *   No. You must still apply and be accepted into the school. There is an application fee, that the school cannot pay, and once you are accepted they pay for the rest of your expenses. This is one reason for the NCAA rule that requires you to provide an official transcript prior to an official visit. This way the school can tell before they offer you a scholarship if you have a legitimate chance of being accepted.

This is the prize in recruiting. Your goal should be to get a scholarship offer from the school you want to attend. If that offer comes, take it and run. If it does not, but other offers do come then I recommend you make your decision based on the following factors.

1. Does the school have your academic program that you would like to study? It's tough to be an architect if the don't have an architecture program.

2. Where is the school located? If you want your family and friends to see you play, will they be able to based on where you want to go?

3. How did you fit in with the players on your visit? The coaching staff may change, but the majority of the players will not.

4. Are you comfortable with how long it will take for you to play there? Some guys will come in and start the first year. Most guys will red-shirt and sit behind a guy for a year or two. Are you being realistic about when you will have a chance to play?

5. How well did you get along with the coaches? In my opinion, this is the least important factor because college coaches are so mobile it is rare for one to be there the entire time you are

at the school. If you do your research, you will see the average coach's tenure at a school is less than they five years you will be there. In the Big 12, in the last five years, eight out of ten schools have changed coaches since 2010. Coaches move for lots of reasons. They get better jobs or they get fired, very few get to retire. This should be a factor in your decision, but not one I would put a lot of weight in.

Chapter 11
Signing Day to Reporting Day

       National Signing Day is so exciting that some student-athletes take the rest of the year off. It is a tough time because you are between teams. You are no longer a member of your high school program and as a result your high school coach does not keep close tabs on you, but you are not yet on the college campus so the college coach has a hard time keeping track of you too. You are a man without a team and in most cases on your own. Many athletes struggle with this, and as a result get out of shape and don't train as hard as they did for their senior year of high school. Some students also struggle academically, too. It's partly Senioritis and partly because there is no accountability to a coach. As a result of this condition I have developed ten things to do between National Signing Day and the day your report for fall camp on campus.

1.   Complete your application packet for the school you just signed a letter of intent to attend.

          Do it right away. There is a deadline, so get your materials in order, your fee together, and get it done. I cannot tell you how many phone calls I have received in the spring from college coaches asking me to remind Johnny to get his stuff turned in so they can get it processed and into school. For whatever reason, some athletes think that by signing a letter of intent they are done, or the school will take care of it, or they don't need to worry about little things like applications. Get it done, and get it done right away.

2.   Go to their Spring Game.

You signed in February, and most spring games are in April. This gives you a chance to get back on campus and make some connections that will make it easier for you to transition in the fall. Call your player-host and ask him if you can sleep on his couch for the weekend and bring a high school buddy along. Have your parents come along and sit with the other parents at the game. This will help them start a network of support for the next five years.

Ask the coaches if you can sit in on the meetings and go to a few practices. This will help you get a feel for what it will be like in the fall and help calm any anxiety about the decision you made a few months earlier. All of the people in those meetings and on the field will be there in August when you arrive so get to know them, they are not going anywhere.

3.   Start their workout plan.

Most colleges will send you an exercise plan after signing day. It will be a booklet of lifts, speed drills, conditioning plans, and flexibility exercises. Read the book, study the book, know the book, do the book. You are getting ready to begin the most physically difficult thing you have done so far in your athletic career. This workout plan will help your chances of being ready.

The biggest difference between a high school practice and a college practice is not the plays or even the players; it's the speed and intensity. When you ran 40-yard sprints with your high school team, it was not a big deal. It may have even been considered an easy day. When you get to college, it is unbelievable how challenging a 40-yard sprint workout can become. You will see athletes throwing up, cramping up, and giving up on the first day. The workout they send you will not get you ready for that, but it will get you a lot closer.

4.   Stretch Every Day.

There are only two ways to get faster, by either increasing your stride frequency or increasing your stride length. Your stride frequency is how quickly you can complete a stride. The shorter time needed, the quicker you can take your strides, the faster you get. This can be helped through plyometrics and ground based power exercises like power cleans, hang cleans, high pulls, etc... Your stride length is increased by your flexibility. The more flexible you are the higher your knee will rise when you are running, the higher your knee goes the longer it's off the ground, the more ground you cover, with fewer strides, the faster you become. The easiest way to get faster is increase your flexibility. In order to do that you should stretch every day.

If you are a serious athlete, you will stretch every day. Do it in the morning, do it at night, do it watching television, just do it. Do it every day and you will be amazed at how much progress you will make in a short amount of time and how much better you will feel. Flexibility plus power equals speed.

5.   Eat Breakfast.

When a college freshman football player comes home at the end of the year, many people are amazed at how much bigger he has become. The say things like, "They must really have you in the weight room up there." There is no doubt they do, but the biggest difference between high school and college is that you are required to go to breakfast every day. Many colleges will have you sign in at breakfast each morning to ensure that you are up and out of bed, and to make sure you are starting out the day with a good meal.

Start that habit now. Make sure you are eating a good breakfast every day. You will find that you will start making gains again in the weight room, you will have more energy, and you will feel better. Start each morning with a bowl of cereal, some fruit, work in an egg or pancake every now and then and you will be thrilled with the results.

6.   Run, Run, Run, and then Run some more.

You cannot get in good enough shape before you go to college. Here is an analogy. It has been a long practice at your high school and you are finishing with a goal line period. Prior to the last play your high school coach announces, "If the offense scores they don't have to condition, and if the defense stops them, then they don't have to condition." The intensity level rises because nobody wants to run at the end of practice. It will be the most intense play of the day and guys that may have been tires a few minutes beforehand have a full tank of gas. That one play, is like every play at a college practice. If you don't go as hard as you possibly can on every single play, there is another player that was recruited to play your position too, who is waiting for his chance. If you will not go hard, then he will. Most high school teams lack competition for each position, colleges do not. There are 25 new guys each fall who are hungry to make an impact, and feel like they deserve a chance to play right now. It will be one of the most competitive situations of your life. You cannot play at that level over an entire practice, without being in phenomenal shape. Fatigue makes cowards of us all, and you cannot run enough before you report to fall camp.

If you come back to your high school during your freshman year you will know what I am talking about. You will look out on the field and ask yourself, "Why aren't these guys trying?" The intensity you have experience on the college campus will make you look at high school football and wonder, why is everyone going so slow. Every player who I have coached has said the same thing when the came back to the high school, "Coach, was I that slow when I played?" The answer is, without a doubt, yes. The intensity of college makes the game so much faster, so be in shape so you can keep up.

7.   Take a Summer Visit.

For the same reason you went to the spring game you should take a week and go on campus and workout with the team. You will see the intensity I am talking about in the workouts and it will give you an opportunity to make some more connections to make the transition to college easier.

Call up your player-host again and see if he will give you a place to stay. Remember the recruiting process is over so bring some money for groceries and entertainment. My roommate and I hosted a player one winter and he came up and stayed with us for a week in the summer. He didn't know the recruiting visit was over and kept going to the fridge for food. In the summer we did not have training table, but we did get stipend to purchase groceries. My roommate and I tried to spend as little as possible on food so we would have more money for entertainment purposes. We determined on about the third day the recruit was penniless and had no intentions of contributing to our food supplies. This did not go over well, and for the next four years we did not let him forget that we thought he was a low-life free loader.

8.   Play in an All-Star Game.

Some D-I recruits will shy away from All-Star Games because they are afraid of getting injured. While that is a legitimate concern, your chances of getting injured in that game are no greater than your chances of getting injured in any other high school game you played in over the last four years. All-Star games are a great way to wrap up your high school career and in most cases are tied to a charity like the Shriner's Hospital. These are fantastic causes that deserve your support and in 99% of the cases you will get more out of playing in the game than they get from you playing.

In addition, it's a lot of fun. Very few high school players get invited to play on an all-star team, even fewer get invited to play on a college all-star team, and fewer still make it all the way to the NFL's Pro Bowl. Enjoy the fact you have been picked as an all-star, help promote our great game, help a worthy cause, and have fun.

9. Focus on your fundamentals.

There are two things you need to be able to do as a football player, depending on what your offensive or defensive focus.

As a defensive player you must:

1. Understand the concept of block protection.

    - Block protection is the process of getting unblocked. As a defensive player there will be an offensive player on every play assigned to prevent you from making the tackle. That offensive player is going to do everything he can to block you out of the play. As a defensive player you have to know how to get rid of the offensive player as quickly as possible. Each defensive position has fundamentals associated with block protection. A defensive lineman will shed a blocker with different fundamentals than a defensive back, your job is to learn those fundamentals and become great at them.

2. Tackle

    - If you can tackle you can play defense. I am not talking about a grab the jersey and hope he falls down tackle. I mean a wrap your arms, bring your hips, explode through the offensive player, and drive him to the ground, tackle. Guys who can do that will always have a place to play on any team. If you want to play defense, you should become a world class tackler.

As an offensive player you must:

1. Understand the concept of ball protection.

- Nobody wants the running back that fumbles, the receiver that cannot catch, or the quarterback that throws the ball to the wrong team. Nobody. Those guys are called "coach killers" because they get guys fired and nobody wants to get fired. If you are an offensive skill player then you should focus on the fundamentals of handling the football. You should become physically sick at the thought of mishandling the football. You should put a football in your bedroom and hold it correctly while you do your homework, do chores around the house, and mow the grass. The first thing you should do at practice everyday is get a ball before warm-ups. Carry a ball around from drill to drill, through stretching and run with it in conditioning. The more you carry this ball correctly the more it will become second nature and the better you are with ball protection fundamentals.

2. Know how to block.

- Every offensive player needs to know how to block, not just the offensive linemen. Know how to block correctly with great footwork, your hand inside the frame, driving your feet, good head placement, in a power position. Know how to block correctly. Offensive lineman should find a head boxing bag and work on coming out of a stance in a power position and getting good hand placement. They should work on the pass sets on air, keeping their head back and their body in a good power position. Think about what fundamentals are essential to being a great blocker at your position and find a way to practice them as much as you can.

Defensive players that can get off blocks and tackle, and offensive players that take care of the football and can block, will always have a place to play.

10.   Read at least one non-academic book a month.

The biggest difference academically between high school and college is the amount of material you will cover each class period and each semester. It is not uncommon to read 100 pages per class per week. If you are enrolled in four or five classes that can add up in a hurry. Too many high school athletes do not read for pleasure. Reading is a chore done when an assignment is given and only done when required. Break that cycle. Go the bookstore or library and find something you are interested in and read it. It can be fiction, non-fiction, science fiction, fantasy, biography, anything you find interesting and read it. Reading is like everything else, you get better at it the more you do it. Practice your reading just like you would anything else and you will find you get better at it in a hurry and it is a great way to relax. In addition, it will help you when you get to college and you have four hundred pages to read in a week. You will be glad you spent part of your senior year improving your reading ability.

Chapter 11
Signing Day to Reporting Day

Enclosed are some motivational messages and letters I have shared with my team that you may enjoy. Recruiting can be a lonely journey and you will need to find things to motivate you every day to keep working and believing in yourself, hopefully some of these may help.

Do Your Habits Match Your Goals?

I believe there are two criteria for setting goals. First, a goal needs to be meaningful. If you set your goal to be the best player you can possibly be on every down next fall, that is a meaningful goal. Second, a goal needs to be realistic. If your goal next fall is to be an all-state player, or a starter, or to get a football scholarship, those are all meaningful goals, but are they realistic. Where does your potential fall? Are you an all-state caliber player? Are you good enough to warrant a college football scholarship? Is a good goal for you to be a starter on your high school team? Or is a better goal to be a contributor on special teams and in practice? We all have a certain ability level that determines what our goals should be, are your goals realistic?

In order to accomplish this meaningful and realistic goal, you need to make sure your habits match your goals. If you really want to be an all-state player, do you work like one? If you really want to get a football scholarship, do you work hard enough in the classroom as well as the weight room? If you really want to make a contribution to your team, do you do what year team needs you to do? Physically do you need to improve your strength, endurance, flexibility, and nutrition? How much work will it take? Are you willing to do what it takes? When are you going to get started?

Everybody wants to be successful. Everyone wants to win. It is easy to say, however, it is much harder to do. If your habits don't match your goals, then one of them needs to change. If you don't want to study, if you don't have time or want to lift, if you don't want to improve your nutrition, then you need to change what you are working towards. Change your goals to something less meaningful, like being competitive in every game or just beating a specific opponent, but who wants to work towards meaningless goals?

I received in the mail a good quote on some recruiting propaganda. It defined the term "Investment" as "The time will come when fall will ask what you were doing all summer." I like that quote, and I believe it is true. The time will pass between now and your first game next season whether you do anything or not. It is what you do between now and then that will determine if you are successful. I also like the quote, "It's not the hours you put in, its what you put into the hours." Don't just go through the motions of strength training, conditioning, speed drills, or studying. Put your whole heart and soul into it and give it 100% of your time, energy, and effort. If you do that, then you will not look back without any regrets because your habits matched your goals.

Hope Is Not A Plan

The biggest thing that has changed since I played high school football is recruiting. The internet has helped to promote players to colleges, and internet recruiting services are the next generation of recruiting. Several years ago an internet service, Rivals100.com held a Junior Day for the top players in Kansas City at Schlagle High School. One of the editors of the web site called me and asked me to talk at the Junior Day. I did it. The next thing I know he asks me to go to Oklahoma City and do the same talk. Over the next couple of years I spoke at Junior Days in Kansas City; Dallas; Lafayette, Louisiana; Houston; Dallas; Columbus, Ohio; Orlando; Nashville; New Orleans; and Columbia, Missouri.

My topic is the recruiting process and how to maximize your opportunities to get a college football scholarship. They also have speakers on nutrition, speed training, and strength training. I like hearing the other speeches to see if there is anything I can do to help my program. One weekend in Houston they had a speaker that played football at Cal and now works as a personal trainer. His name is Sean Adams. In his speech he talked about how "hope is not a plan." He talked about how if you want to be an athlete you have to train like an athlete, and most importantly we need to make sure we have a plan to improve.

Hope is not a plan. Sometimes you hear a phrase or a quote and it makes sense to you. Hope is not a plan. This makes sense to me. If you want to be good at something you have to do more than just hope that it will happen. This not only applies to athletics but also academics. If you want to score well on an upcoming test or project in one of your classes, you have to do more than just hope it happens. If you have homework, you have to more than just hope that it gets done. If you want to have a successful season next year, you have to more than just hope that it happens.

What is your plan? Take some time and write it down on paper. What are you specifically going to do to make sure that you reach your goals? Here are some things to consider when making your plan.

1. When football is over, are you going to go out for another sport? If you are wondering if you should, I recommend you go for it. Multi-sport athletes are usually great competitors and better athletes than athletes that focus on only one thing. You work different muscle groups in different sports, and you learn how to work with different people to be a team. If you chose to not go out for other sports then how many days a week do you need to train to be successful?

2. What program are you going to use to improve? If you are making it up, your chances of making big gains are less likely than if you use a proven program. Ask your high school coach or college coach on what he recommends; he should be able to help. If that is not an option, go the library or search the internet to find something that can help you improve.

3. How important is making money or having a car? Some high school kids get so caught up in having a few bucks in their pocket or having a car they get jobs where they work 20 hours a week. If you factor in seven hours of school a day, five days a week, for a total of 35 hours a week at school, and put a part-time job that adds another 20 hours a week to an already full week. There is 55 hours a week on work and school, throw on top of that homework and a social life and it's easy to see how strength and speed training get pushed off the schedule. Can you live without the spending money and car? Some kids have to work to help their family; however, most kids do not fall into that category. Most kids are working for spending money, car insurance, gasoline, and new sneakers. Can you live without those things so you can have the time to commit to improving as an athlete?

4. How can you make yourself accountable to your plan? The best way to do this is to have a training partner. If you don't feel like working out some days, he will, and vise versa. It also makes it more fun to train with someone. People are social animals and companionship

makes training easier. If that is not an option then share your plan with your parents and ask them to encourage you to follow through. Sometimes it improves your accountability if other people know that you have a plan and you should be training to improve.

Hope is not a plan. You have to do more than just hope you will get better. You have to do more than just hope you will be good enough to be an all-state player. You have to have a plan and you have to work that plan, and leave hope out of it.

More than Want To

The idea of an off-season sounds like it should be a time of leisure. The off-season used to be a time when you could rest your body and when practice started in the fall you worked your way into shape. Some schools still do it that way, however those schools don't win much. Good programs realize the only difference between the season and the off-season is whether or not you wear equipment. Good programs realize the off-season is our time to improve. Good programs win games in the off-season.

My college coach, Glen Mason, used to say, "Each day you either get better or you get worse, you never stay the same." He used to say it all the time. As a player I didn't want to believe it. I wanted to be able to take a day off and still be as good as I was the day before. I understand the temptation. However, I want to win. Furthermore, I understand what it takes to win. I also understand that every one of our opponents also wants to win, and they are going to be using their time to improve as well. If you show up next fall and have not improved from last year, you will not win.

You need to make a commitment to improvement. You must first realize you will not get better by simply wanting to improve, then realize what you need to improve, make a plan, and work their plan. Improvement is a slow process and if you get a little better every day, then over time you will make huge gains. For example, if you can improve your bench by five pounds a month, a little more than a pound a week, if you do that over an eight month period you would make a 40 lbs jump. You could go from a 200 lbs. bench to a 240 lbs. bench. If you improve your 40 yard dash by .02 seconds a month, you could improve your time from a 5.0 to 4.84. Big gains, made a little at a time. It's not easy to do, it takes great patience and commitment, but it's done every year by somebody. Will it be you? Wanting to improve is not enough. If you do not improve, you will not win.

I am glad it's not easy. Most things in life that are easy are not rewarding. If it were easy then everyone could do it, but it's not. What would it be like if your school won the state championship? What would it feel like? How would your community treat you if we were able to accomplish that incredible goal? You will determine in the next few months how your fall will go next year. If you make a commitment to improve, the only limits you will have will be the ones you place on yourselves. It can happen, but you have to do more than just want it to happen, you have to make it happen every day!

How Tough is Tough Enough?

How tough are you? This is a question commonly asked by coaches to players. It is far and away the most commonly asked question by college coaches about senior football players they are recruiting. I went to the University of Iowa football clinic recently and heard their defensive coordinator, Norm Parker, talk about defense. He started his talk by saying, "You know the longer I am in coaching the more I realize that toughness is the single most important thing I look for in a player." My coach at Kansas, current University of Minnesota coach Glen Mason, used to say, "If you are ever going to be any good at this game you have to be one tough sucker!" I heard him say it a million times.

Why is toughness so important in football? Why do all of these highly successful coaches talk about it all the time? What is it about being a tough guy that makes you a good football player? The answer is simple; football is a tough game to play. It is played in the heat, the cold, the rain, and the snow. It is played with sophisticated equipment to protect your body from violent collisions. It takes physical strength and great endurance. It requires year-round preparation to play one season. It is so taxing, we only play once a week to allow your body and spirit can recover. So, are you tough enough?

What does toughness look like? Where does toughness come from? How can a player improve his toughness? The biggest misconception players have is that toughness is something you are born with and never develop. A guy is either tough or he is not, and there is not a middle ground. I don't think that is true. Toughness is developed by how you deal with pain and is determined by your attitude. There is a lot of pain in football. When you are running 100 yard sprints in the summer, it hurts. When you have one more set of front squats and your legs are burning, it hurts. When you are running hills in the summer, it hurts. When the alarm clock goes off at 5:30 a.m. in the summer and you have to workout, it hurts. When you get to the last set of your dumbbell complex, it hurts. When it is 95 degrees outside and you are putting on your helmet to go out to practice for two hours, it hurts. And when you come up one point short against your biggest rival, it hurts more than anything. The next time you feel one of those pains, say this to yourself, "I am tough enough." Another 100 yard sprint, I am tough enough; another set of front squats, I am tough enough; another hill to run, I am tough enough; 5:30 a.m. and it's time to go, I am tough enough; last set of dumbbells, I am tough enough; fourth quarter against our biggest rival, I know I am tough enough!

You will be amazed at how tough you will become if every time you feel the pain you answer it with your attitude. Toughness is not genetic. Toughness does not come from the outside in, but rather the inside out. Toughness is developed every day, and how tough you are is exposed every day. A tough guy battles through conditioning drills, he battles though injuries, he battles through the pain associated with playing this game. He understands there is no greater honor in football than being considered a tough guy and he looks for the toughness of his teammates. Developing toughness as individuals will develop toughness as a team, and that will take your team to the next level.

Teammates

What does it take to be a team? How do you become a team? Why is it that some groups of athletes never become a team? Have you ever asked yourself these questions? Coaches have for years. There are hundreds of books written on teamwork. Businesses use sports analogies all the time to get their employees to think like a team, act like a team, and work like a team. Right now there are football coaches all around the state and country wondering, "Will I have a team next fall or a group of individuals?"

Webster's on-line dictionary says:

Main Entry: ³**team**
Function: *adjective*
: of or performed by a team <a *team* effort>; *also*: marked
by devotion to teamwork rather than individual
achievement <a *team* player>

Main Entry: **team work**
Pronunciation: 'tEm-"w&rk
Function: *noun*
: work done by several associates with each doing a part
but all subordinating personal prominence to the
efficiency of the whole

Teams are made of teammates. Groups are made of individuals.
If you asked 10 people what a team looks like, nine of them would say
exactly what Webster says, a group working together for a common cause.
However, that's not teamwork, that's cooperation. Teamwork is based on
service. A true team is made up of individuals that care more about one
another than they do themselves. They care less about records, playing
time, and recognition and more about earning the loyalty and respect of
their teammates. They look to build one another up, encourage one
another, and serve one another. Most teams miss this point.

The enemy of every group trying to become a team is selfishness.
When coaches and players start to think more what they are getting out of
being on the team rather than what contribution they can make, the team
starts to fail. When coaches and players value recognition and individual
honors and responsibilities over the team, the group stays a group rather
than becoming a team. A teammate thinks differently. He talks about
what is good for the team. He cares about what his teammates say about
his toughness, his work ethic, and his attitude. He contributes every day
to the morale and spirit of the group. He looks for guys having a tough
day and builds them up rather than complain about them not pulling their
weight. They look for opportunities to build bridges with their teammates
and avoid building fences to separate the team. The most important thing
to them is being a member of the team, and they care about every player
and coach on the team.

Nobody works all year to lose. Nobody goes into the weight room
with the goal of mediocrity. I challenge each of you to find ways to be
teammates. Encourage one another to prepare for the season, sacrifice
your ego for our team's success, and look for the toughness, work ethic,
and attitude in one another.

The Hay is in the Barn

"The hay is in the barn." Before the first game of my coaching career the head coach leaned over and said that to me as we walked to the field. It was at Eudora Middle school prior to our 7th grade game, and I smiled and nodded and had no idea what he was talking about. It was in a small town of 3600 in Kansas and he figured that since I was an Iowa boy I would know the farm lingo. I didn't. I can remember thinking, yeah the cow is in the field and horse is in the stable, what's your point? I later learned that what he meant was, the work is done and now it's time to play.

Have you ever studied so hard for a big test that when you showed up to take the test you were so tired of the material you didn't even want to read the questions? Sometimes the same thing happens in sports. We work so hard all year that we take the season for granted. Most high school teams play about 10 regular season football games, some teams are good enough to make it to the playoffs and may play as many as 14 games, regardless if your team plays 10 games or 14 games, you will have put a lot of hours into those games. My college offensive line coach put it like this: the average offensive play lasts 5 seconds, and the average offense runs about 75 plays a game, so you really only play 375 seconds a game, or 6 minutes and 15 seconds. Take that times 10 games and you play a little more than an hour a year.

How hard do you play? Do you go as hard as you can on every down, or are you saving something for the next play? If you only get to play for 6 minutes and 15 seconds a week, could you go harder? Most players can. If you go on to college football and then come back and watch a high school game you will be amazed at how slow the game looks. It looks like everyone is going about half speed and they are not really trying. I have talked to players that have gone on to college and come back to watch their high school team play and ask, "Was I that slow when I player?" The answer is absolutely. The college game is faster for several reasons. The players are faster, but that is not the biggest reason, the biggest reason is competition. Most college players have earned their position through a tough battle with another player and if they don't perform at a high level the coach will put the other player in the game. Most high school teams lack competition for positions. Star players don't have to go as hard as they can to keep their spot and as a result the game is slower.

How hard can you play every down? If you don't have another player pushing you for your position, then push yourself. When it is Friday night and you are playing under the lights, give it your 100%. Don't play at the speed of the game, play at your top speed on every down. You only get so many plays in your career, don't take one off. When you get a chance to perform, give it all you got. After you have worked all summer and lifted all those weights all year, and the "Hay is in the Barn", go put on a show on Friday nights.

Potions, Pills, and Magic

"Coach, should I take Creatine?" It seems like I am asked this question more often each year. As pro athletes become more involved in sports supplements, we in the high school world will be exposed to this more. We hear about Tim Dwight, Bill Romanowski, Shannon Sharp and other highly successful pros attribute their success to supplements, and we naturally think that if it works for them it will work for us. I did not use anything like that when I played; I never had any trouble gaining weight or strength, so I have always advised players against using them. However, each year I felt less and less comfortable with my thinking so I decided to do some research, and here is what I found.

Nutritionist and sports trainers both recommend the same diet for athletes as non-athletes. A healthy person should monitor their caloric intake based on their desired weight. On the back of this sheet is a chart to help you out. Find your desired weight. Let's use the example of 200 pounds. There are three different numbers of calories for that weight. For a sedentary person it is 2200 calories, for a person that exercises at a moderate level it is 2600 calories, and for a person that is active it is 3000 calories. The more you exercise, the more you can eat at each weight. Hopefully all of you fall in the active category since we are training for next season. Now out of those calories you should devote 60% to carbohydrates, 25% to fat, and 15% to protein. If you go across on the chart for an active 200-pound person you should take in 450 grams of carbohydrates, 113 grams of protein, and 83 grams of fat. This is recommended in all of the articles, textbooks, and sports supplement literature I read.

The next thing I did was to put together a healthy eating program for a high school player and see if he needed to supplement his diet. Look at the sample diet on the back of this page. When I figured out what three good meals, a snack after school, and a snack before bed did for his nutrition, I was surprised. I looked up how many grams of protein, carbohydrates, and fat were in each food on the website www.caloriechart.org. This person met all his needs for carbohydrates, protein, and fat. Does he need to supplement his diet? No. By eating three good meals and two snacks he exceeded the amount of protein he needs. Research shows that your body will not utilize the protein if you exceed more than 1 gram per pound of body weight. In other words, if our 200 pound person takes in more than 200 grams of protein, it will be stored as fat. That is not what you want.

Creatine is an amino acid. I read in a textbook, "A diet containing large amounts of protein will **_not_** support growth, repairs, and maintenance of tissues **_if_** the essential amino acids are not available in proper proportions. Most of the proteins from animal foods contain all the essential amino acids that humans require." In other words, if you eat a healthy diet it will meet your needs for protein and amino acids, allowing your body to build lean muscle. If you want to make the most of your strength training, the next step is to commit yourself to balanced, healthy diet. If you are trying to build your body into a powerful weapon, you want to use the best materials available. If you think you should be taking a supplement do two things. First, write down your diet and look up where you are at without a supplement and see if you need one. Second, see you family doctor and see what he thinks. He will know what is best for your body.

"If it sounds too good to be true, it usually is." I am sure you have heard that expression. I wish there were some potion, pill, or magic that would allow us to be successful. We could hold a fundraiser and buy a state championship. We could distribute the potion to each player that wants to be on our team and manufacture a group of supermen. We would beat everyone by 49 points. However, there is no such thing, and I am glad. I think the best part of building a program is the process along the way, and success should not come easy. If being successful were easy, the world would be filled successful people. It is not. If you want to be successful you have to be different. You have to be willing to work in the weight room, eat right, get your rest, and put it on the line every Friday night. If you do that, you will not need any potions, pills, or magic, all we will need is your ring size.

Food	Fat	Carbs	Protein
Breakfast			
3 Scrambled Eggs	15	5	18
1 Piece of Cheese	9	0	7
2 Pieces of Toast	2	24	4
1 Glass of Orange Juice	0	26	2
1 Pat of Butter	4	0	0
2 Cartons of Milk (Size you get at Lunch)	0	56	18
Lunch			
Turkey Sandwich			
2 Slices of Bread	2	24	4
2 Slices of Turkey	1	0	10
1 Piece of Cheese	9	0	7
Lettuce & Tomato	0	1	0
1 Tablespoon Mayo	5	4	0
1 Bag of Pretzels	0	4	0
2 Cartons of Chocolate Milk	0	56	18
2 Cartons of Fruit Drink	0	30	0
Snack			
2.5 oz Beef Jerky	4	0	24
Apple	0	16	0
2 Cartons of Fruit Drink	0	30	0
Dinner			
1 Pork Chop	8	0	23
1 Baked Potato	0	51	5
1 Pat of Butter	4	0	0
Salad	0	4	2
2 Tablespoon Ranch Dressing	4	4	0
Snack			
Peanut Butter & Jelly Sandwich			
2 Slices of Bread	2	24	4
1 Tablespoon Peanut Butter	8	3	5
1 Tablespoon Jelly	0	14	0
Apple	0	16	0
2 Cartons of Chocolate Milk	0	56	18
Totals	77	448	169

Calories Needed

Desired Weight	Sedentary Exercise	Moderate Exercise	Active Exercise
100	1100	1300	1500
110	1210	1430	1650
120	1320	1560	1800
130	1430	1690	1950
140	1540	1820	2100
150	1650	1950	2250
160	1760	2080	2400
170	1870	2210	2550
180	1980	2340	2700
190	2090	2470	2850
200	2200	2600	3000
210	2310	2730	3150
220	2420	2860	3300
230	2530	2990	3450
240	2640	3120	3600
250	2750	3250	3750
260	2860	3380	3900
270	2970	3510	4050
280	3080	3640	4200
290	3190	3770	4350

Sedentary Lifestyle

Sedentary			
Desired Weight	Grams of Carbs	Grams of Protein	Grams of Fat
100	165	41	31
110	182	45	34
120	198	50	37
130	215	54	40
140	231	58	43
150	248	62	46
160	264	66	49
170	281	70	52
180	297	74	55
190	314	78	58
200	330	83	61
210	347	87	64
220	363	91	67
230	380	95	70
240	396	99	73
250	413	103	76
260	429	107	79
270	446	111	83
280	462	116	86
290	479	120	89

Moderate Exercise Lifestyle

	Moderate		
Desired Weight	Grams of Carbs	Grams of Protein	Grams of Fat
100	195	49	36
110	215	54	40
120	234	59	43
130	254	63	47
140	273	68	51
150	293	73	54
160	312	78	58
170	332	83	61
180	351	88	65
190	371	93	69
200	390	98	72
210	410	102	76
220	429	107	79
230	449	112	83
240	468	117	87
250	488	122	90
260	507	127	94
270	527	132	98
280	546	137	101
290	566	141	105

Active Lifestyle

	Active		
Desired Weight	Grams of Carbs	Grams of Protein	Grams of Fat
100	225	56	42
110	248	62	46
120	270	68	50
130	293	73	54
140	315	79	58
150	338	84	63
160	360	90	67
170	383	96	71
180	405	101	75
190	428	107	79
200	450	113	83
210	473	118	88
220	495	124	92
230	518	129	96
240	540	135	100
250	563	141	104
260	585	146	108
270	608	152	113
280	630	158	117
290	653	163	121

Made in the USA
San Bernardino, CA
31 December 2015